Countdown to Winning Bridge

Countdown to Winning Bridge

Tim Bourke & Marc Smith

MASTER POINT PRESS
TORONTO

© 1999 Tim Bourke and Marc Smith

Master Point Press
22 Lower Village Gate
Toronto, Ontario Canada
M5P 3L7
(416) 932-9766
Internet www.pathcom.com/~raylee/

Distributed in the USA by Barricade Books
150 Fifth Avenue, Suite 700
New York, NY 10011
(800) 59-BOOKS

Canadian Cataloguing in Publication Data
Bourke, Tim
Countdown to winning bridge

ISBN 1-894154-05-3

1. Contract bridge — Defensive play. 2. Contract bridge — Dummy play.
I. Smith, Marc, 1960-   II. Title.

GV1282.42.B68 1999   795.41'53   C98-932698-5

| *Editor* | Ray Lee |
| *Cover and Interior design* | Olena S. Sullivan |

Printed and bound in Canada

1 2 3 4 5 6 7   06 05 04 03 02 01 00 99

Foreword

When it comes to card play and defense, what edge do the top players have? Card sense and flair, perhaps? Fortunately for the majority of players, the true answer is less romantic — they achieve their fine results mainly by hard work. To determine the best line of play or the best defense, the essential first step is to gather information on the closed hands. Only when you have a picture of all four hands will the right line of play become apparent.

In this excellent book, Tim Bourke and Marc Smith show how you can 'count the hand', discovering the shape of the closed hands and the location of the key high cards. They explain clearly the latest methods of signalling, which allow defenders to give each other an early count. There are also plenty of realistic examples, many from championship play, to demonstrate how you can take advantage of the information gained.

If you have been playing bridge without counting the hand, perhaps for many years, you are about to enter a new world! Plays and defenses that were previously out of reach will become part of your standard repertoire. You will have to put in some hard work along the way, it's true, but the dramatic improvement in your play will make it all worthwhile.

DAVID BIRD

Acknowledgments

The authors wish to thank the following people for their assistance: Maureen Dennison, Andrew Southwell, Julian Pottage, Charlotte Smith and all the monks at St.Titus for their diligent proofreading; Ray Lee at Master Point Press for his editing skills; and our wives, Charlotte Smith and Margi Bourke, for their incredible patience.

Thanks also to Matthew Granovetter for permitting us to use part of an article that first appeared in *Bridge Today*.

Contents

SECTION 1

The Basics

Experienced players might prefer to skim or even bypass this first section, in which we focus primarily on the actual mechanics of counting. From there on, they'll find all the challenge they can wish for. However, having said that, we suspect even those players might find some of the tips in the early chapters useful, and they probably shouldn't ignore them completely.

CHAPTER 1

Why Count?

o you remember sitting behind the wheel of a car for your first driving lesson? Like us, you probably wondered how you were supposed to watch the traffic while simultaneously making the car go where you wanted it to, let alone worrying about how you switched on the wipers or the turn signal. For many bridge players, the word 'counting' seems to evoke similar feelings of confusion and dread. This is particularly curious, since even small children can count to thirteen. The good news is that, with practice, counting at the bridge table can become as routine as driving a car or riding the proverbial bike. In this chapter, we'll also show you how useful a skill it is to acquire.

When you first started playing bridge, you probably found that you often seemed to freeze because there were so many things to think about that you did not know where to start. You had to count high card points and remember to add distributional points which, you were told, changed as the bidding progressed. You also had to work out how many points partner's bid showed and add them to your own. It is little wonder that, by the time dummy appeared, you had precious little energy left to count your winners and losers, let alone remember how many trumps were out. Fairly soon, though, you were able to keep a running total of the number of trumps played as a matter of habit. From there it was a small step to work out how many were outstanding — and your counting career had begun.

Counting during the play of the hand takes many forms. Keeping track of the number of trumps played is where we all start. As we gain experience, we learn to pay attention to the cards played in more than one suit, so that we know whether, for example, dummy's remaining low diamond is a winner. Having mastered these basic counting tasks, we learn to count the opponents' hands too. In this book, we start at the very beginning by looking at *how* you should count — by using patterns. As we progress, so the hands become progressively more difficult. Even players with very little experience should have no trouble with our first hand; however, it allows us to introduce some useful ideas:

N-S Vul.	♠	K Q 5 4
Lead: ♣K	♥	K 8 3
	♦	8 6
	♣	A 9 4 2

	♠	A 7 2
	♥	A Q 5 4
	♦	A K Q J 2
	♣	J

WEST	NORTH	EAST	SOUTH
	1♣	pass	1♦
pass	1♠	pass	4NT
pass	5♦	pass	5NT
pass	6♥	pass	7NT
all pass			

You must train yourself to count your tricks, even in simple contracts. This is something we are all taught as novices, and it is a process that even the expert player performs on every hand. Here you have eleven top tricks — one club, four diamonds, three hearts and three spades, so you must find two more to bring your total to thirteen. Your twelfth trick, you hope, will come from the fifth diamond in hand and the thirteenth from a 3-3 break in one of the majors. (More experienced readers will have noticed squeeze chances, but we are ignoring them on this hand in the interest of emphasizing the mechanics of the counting process).

West leads the ♣K, so you win the ♣A and immediately test diamonds. The skill you have acquired in counting trumps will make keeping an eye on the diamond suit a breeze, but it is worth mentioning quickly exactly *how* you should count the defenders' diamonds.

Deducting your seven diamonds from thirteen tells you the defenders have six diamonds. Although counting to six may not seem overly arduous, it's still easier to think in terms of suit combinations. In this instance, the defenders' diamonds may break 3-3, 4-2, 5-1 or 6-0. Both defenders follow to the first diamond winner, so you can rule out the 6-0 breaks. When you cash the second top diamond, everyone follows again. As the suit must now break either 3-3 or 4-2, you don't care who has the remaining diamonds. Rather than counting to thirteen, or even to six, you only had to count to two!

Now that your long diamond is a winner, you have twelve tricks and just need to find one major breaking favorably. How should you proceed? Moderately experienced players would cash the diamond tricks, throwing clubs from dummy, while keeping track of any major-suit discards. Perhaps you note that the defenders have six cards in each major, and as each major-suit card is played you mentally reduce the number of outstanding cards.

Until it becomes a habit, keeping track of both suits may be too much — it is also unnecessary. Choose one of the majors to watch — let's say hearts. After cashing your diamonds, play off the top hearts. Because you have been counting the suit you will know whether the thirteenth heart is a winner. If it is, your problems are over. Otherwise, play four rounds of spades and hope for the best.

With practice, these basic counting processes become routine. After progressing beyond the beginner stage, most players carry them out without conscious thought. The next step in learning to count a bridge hand is to work out the distribution of an opponent's hand. To appreciate the advantages of doing so, try playing a few hands with the defenders' hands face-up on the table like extra dummies.

When you first try to count a defender's shape it seems like an impossible task, even though all the information is in your head. As with most things though, it is only a question of practice. Let's begin with a straightforward example to outline the thought processes you need to follow. If you are feeling industrious, take the South seat and cover the East-West hands.

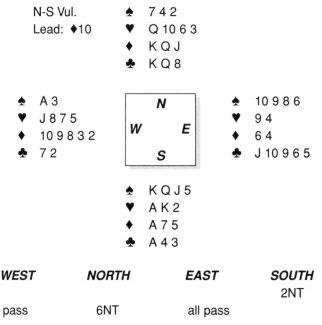

N-S Vul.
Lead: ♦10

North hand:
♠ 7 4 2
♥ Q 10 6 3
♦ K Q J
♣ K Q 8

West hand:
♠ A 3
♥ J 8 7 5
♦ 10 9 8 3 2
♣ 7 2

East hand:
♠ 10 9 8 6
♥ 9 4
♦ 6 4
♣ J 10 9 6 5

South hand:
♠ K Q J 5
♥ A K 2
♦ A 7 5
♣ A 4 3

WEST	NORTH	EAST	SOUTH
			2NT
pass	6NT	all pass	

As always, count your tricks before playing a card. Make a point of doing this on every hand and it will soon become a habit. Here you can count three diamond tricks, three clubs and three hearts on top. Driving out the ♠A will develop two spade tricks. That makes eleven tricks, so you need to find one more. The extra trick must come from spades or hearts.

Now it's time to play. You win the diamond lead in dummy and play a spade to the king, which loses to West's ace. After winning the diamond continuation, it is time to cash some winners to see what you can discover. Start by taking the top spades — if the suit breaks 3-3 you will have twelve tricks. Count the spades by watching to see if everyone follows to three rounds. (Remember that it is easier to count to three than to six.)

West discards a diamond on the third round of spades, and you have reached the next point at which you should pause for thought. As the spades have not broken, your twelfth trick will have to come from hearts. Should you play the three top hearts and hope the suit breaks 3-3, or cash the ace and king and finesse against the jack?

The answer is that it is too early to decide yet. There is still information available that may help you make that decision. For now, fix the spade division in your mind — the defender on your left had only two.

You play off your minor-suit winners and East shows out on the third diamond. That means there were originally five diamonds on your left, so you know seven of West's cards — five diamonds and two spades. You cash your club winners, and when West discards a diamond on the third round, you are almost home. All that remains is to count to thirteen.

West began with two spades, five diamonds and two clubs — that's nine cards that are not hearts — and, therefore, four hearts. It is now easy to cash the ♥AK and, if the jack has not fallen, to play a heart to the ten *knowing* your finesse will win. You could just as easily have counted East's hand — four spades, two diamonds, five clubs (eleven non-hearts) and so only room for two hearts. Note that you need only count one defender's hand. Trying to count both hands not only leads to mistakes but wastes valuable mental energy.

On the last hand, you were able to get an exact count of the defenders' distribution. This will not always be possible, but that does not mean that a little discovery work will not pay handsome dividends. The next hand illustrates why any counting is better than none. If it's not too early in the day, take over from declarer and cover the defenders' hands.

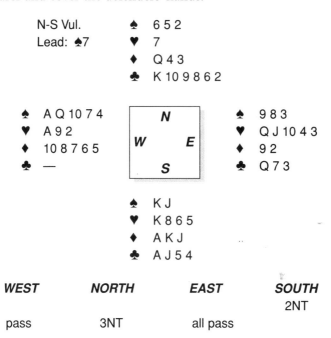

N-S Vul.
Lead: ♠7

North
♠ 6 5 2
♥ 7
♦ Q 4 3
♣ K 10 9 8 6 2

West
♠ A Q 10 7 4
♥ A 9 2
♦ 10 8 7 6 5
♣ —

East
♠ 9 8 3
♥ Q J 10 4 3
♦ 9 2
♣ Q 7 3

South
♠ K J
♥ K 8 6 5
♦ A K J
♣ A J 5 4

WEST	NORTH	EAST	SOUTH
			2NT
pass	3NT	all pass	

The lead is the ♠7, and you win the ♠J as East follows with the three (the lowest missing card in the suit, suggesting an odd number of spades). Stop to count your tricks — one spade, three diamonds and (you hope) six clubs, which is plenty. Clearly, if the missing clubs break 2-1 there is no problem. The only

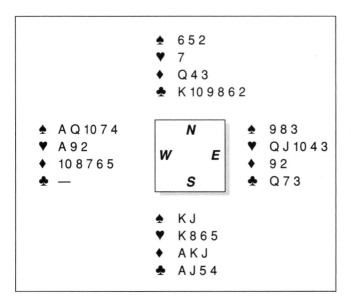

	♠ 6 5 2	
	♥ 7	
	♦ Q 4 3	
	♣ K 10 9 8 6 2	

Diagram repeated for convenience

♠ A Q 10 7 4		♠ 9 8 3
♥ A 9 2	N	♥ Q J 10 4 3
♦ 10 8 7 6 5	W E	♦ 9 2
♣ —	S	♣ Q 7 3

	♠ K J	
	♥ K 8 6 5	
	♦ A K J	
	♣ A J 5 4	

danger is a 3-0 club break. So, which defender is most likely to have a club void?

Based on the lead, perhaps you decide that West has five spades to East's three, so he is more likely to be short in clubs. This in itself is true, but what if North had somehow become declarer and East had led his longest suit — maybe hearts — and he proved to have five of those. Would that make him more likely to be short in clubs? Not really. In both situations, the leader led his longest suit, which is hardly surprising, and you should be cautious about reading too much into that information. (We shall discuss this trap further in Chapter 6.)

So, is it a complete guess? Perhaps, but you do have one opportunity to gain more information before putting your eggs in one basket or the other — you can cash your diamond winners. Eureka! East discards a heart on the third round of diamonds. Your contract is now guaranteed. West started with five diamonds and, presumably, five spades. What are the chances he also has three clubs? None, for then East would have passed as dealer, not vulnerable, with eight hearts to the ace-queen-jack-ten! Your thoughtful play is rewarded when you lead a low club towards dummy and West discards. It is now a simple matter to finesse against East's ♣Q on the way back and claim your contract.

Counting the defenders' hands is crucial to sound declarer play. The more you know about how the opponents' cards lie, the better your decisions will be. Try your hand at the following problem:

N-S Vul.　　　　♠　A J 10
Lead: ♦J　　　　♥　Q J 4 3
　　　　　　　　♦　A K 4
　　　　　　　　♣　A 5 4

```
        N
   W         E
        S
```

　　　　　♠　K 7 3
　　　　　♥　A K 8 5
　　　　　♦　Q 6 2
　　　　　♣　K 3 2

WEST	NORTH	EAST	SOUTH
		pass	1NT
pass	6NT	all pass	

You have eleven top tricks and your contract hinges on locating the ♠Q. With no knowledge of the distribution, this is a 50-50 guess. Can you think of a way to improve those odds?

Initially, both defenders are equally likely to hold the ♠Q. Those odds will alter if the exact distribution of the spade suit is known. The defender with more spades is more likely to hold the queen:

Spades held	Chance of holding the queen
4	4/7 = 57.1%
5	5/7 = 71.4%
6	6/7 = 85.7%
7	7/7 = 100%

Let's see what you can find out. You win the diamond lead and cash your hearts, noting that West follows only twice. Perhaps you decide that West has only two hearts (and thus eleven non-hearts) to East's three, so West is more likely to hold the vital ♠Q. This reasoning is correct, but it would be premature to play a spade to dummy's ten as you have not yet completed all your discovery work.

Can you find out more about the defenders' hands? For example, wouldn't it be nice to know how clubs divide? To do this you must first duck a club — you have to lose a trick at some point anyway. You win the diamond return and play off your minor-suit winners. On the third round of diamonds, East discards a spade, so you now know that West began with seven red cards (two hearts and five diamonds). When you cash the ♣AK, your forethought is rewarded because East discards another spade. Note that it is only because you ducked a club earlier that you were able to see three rounds of the suit.

You now know twelve of West's cards — two hearts, five diamonds and five clubs. It is a simple matter to play a spade to dummy's ace and run the jack on the way back, assured that your finesse will win. This is the full layout:

```
                    ♠  A J 10
                    ♥  Q J 4 3
                    ♦  A K 4
                    ♣  A 5 4

     ♠  9              ┌─────────┐        ♠  Q 8 6 5 4 2
     ♥  9 7            │    N    │        ♥  10 6 2
     ♦  J 10 9 8 3     │ W     E │        ♦  7 5
     ♣  Q 9 8 7 6      │    S    │        ♣  J 10
                       └─────────┘

                    ♠  K 7 3
                    ♥  A K 8 5
                    ♦  Q 6 2
                    ♣  K 3 2
```

This hand provides an insight into why successful players are often known as lucky guessers. What started out as a 50-50 contract became a 100% certainty by the time the critical finesse was taken. Was it so hard? Did you do anything more complicated than count to thirteen?

LESSONS FROM THIS CHAPTER

- **Always** count your tricks before you play to trick one.

- Count missing cards by watching how suits break.

- Knowing the shape of the closed hands is an enormous advantage. Use your counting to work out *one* defender's shape.

- The defender with more cards in a suit is more likely to hold a specific card in that suit.

- The more tricks you play (and thus the more defenders' cards you see) before making a crucial decision, the more likely you are to 'guess' right.

CHAPTER 2

The Mechanics of Counting

'How do you count to thirteen?' This may seem like a silly question, but in this chapter we shall try to persuade you that there are better ways of doing it than the obvious 'one, two, three... twelve, thirteen.'

Keeping track of trumps is a skill novices learn very early. In the beginning, most players figure out if they have drawn trumps by tallying dead cards — cards that have been played. They play a round of trumps and, if everyone follows, count that four have gone. They then add the number of trumps left in their hand and dummy, and if the total is less than thirteen they know some trumps are still outstanding. They repeat the same process after a second round of trumps, and so on. No one can say that this method does not work, but it is tediously slow and uses a great deal of mental energy.

Think of the brain as a fuel tank. When you sit down to play it is full, but every time you make a conscious thought, you burn fuel. As the session wears on, you deplete your reserves of mental energy. To preserve fuel for when you really need to think, you must train yourself to handle routine processes in a way that conserves your mental energy. The first step is to make these basic functions a habit — something you just do without actively thinking about them.

Rather than counting dead cards in a suit, it is more efficient to count live ones. Say, for example, you have seven clubs between your hand and dummy. There is no need to count all thirteen clubs as they are played. It is easier to work out that the opponents started with six clubs, and to reduce that number as clubs are played. You may not need to be Einstein to count to thirteen, but even so, you are even less likely to make a careless error counting to six.

This technique works reasonably well for counting a single suit. It is less effective for determining the distribution of the hidden hands. In order to keep track of more than one suit comfortably, or to envision a defender's hand during the play, you must think in terms of hand patterns and suit distributions. Let's change the subject briefly and consider a bidding problem. Your hand is:

♠ K J 10
♥ —
♦ Q 10 3 2
♣ A Q 10 8 6

You open 1♣ and partner responds 1♠. Do you rebid your clubs or raise partner's spades?

Some of you will have correctly refused to answer, having seen that you were given only twelve cards. If you didn't notice that, it is because you are thinking of a hand as thirteen individual cards rather than as a total hand pattern. Once you begin to think in terms of hand shape, you will be able to eliminate actual counting as suits are played.

During the bidding, the distribution of a hand is often as important as its high-card strength. You should, therefore, consider the shape of your hand from the moment you pick up your cards. Hand patterns are commonly expressed in figures such as 4-4-3-2 or 3-5-3-2 with the suits in their ranking order (spades first, then hearts, diamonds and clubs). Thus, a 4-4-3-2 hand has four spades, four hearts, three diamonds and two clubs. (When a hand pattern is expressed as 4432, without the hyphens, it means you have two four-card suits, a three-card suit and a doubleton, but that the suits are not defined.)

Once you are used to thinking in this way, you will know instinctively if the suit lengths do not add up to thirteen (such as the 3-0-4-5 hand above). When the various hand patterns become familiar, you will also be able to think of individual suits in similar terms. For example, if you are dealt two suits of exactly four cards your only possible shapes are 4432, 4441 and 4450. Similarly, if you have a four-four trump fit, the missing cards can only split 3-2, 4-1 or 5-0. Using this approach, you will find it easier both to keep track of how many cards are outstanding in a suit, and to build up information about the defenders' hands.

You are now ready to test your new counting method. The question is, exactly what should you be counting? Let's answer this with a straightforward hand on which we can work through the thought processes you should follow:

Both Vul.	♠ J 6 3
Lead: ♥5	♥ K J 7 3
	♦ K 7 4 2
	♣ A 7

```
        N
    W       E
        S
```

♠ A Q
♥ A Q 9 6 4
♦ A Q 6
♣ K 9 3

WEST	NORTH	EAST	SOUTH
			1♥
pass	3NT[1]	pass	4NT[2]
pass	5♥[3]	pass	7♥
all pass			

1. Balanced raise to 4♥
2. Roman Key Card Blackwood
3. Two key cards, no ♥Q.

Even on the simplest of hands there is counting to be done, but exactly what should you be counting? At the beginning of each hand, you must count your tricks. This dummy is disappointing as you can only count twelve tricks — five trumps, three diamonds, two clubs, one spade and a club ruff in dummy. However, there are two obvious chances for an extra trick — diamonds might break 3-3 or the spade finesse may work.

Your next task is to develop what we shall call an 'Information Management Strategy' (hereafter referred to as IMS). This may sound complicated and a trifle grandiose, but the name describes exactly what you are trying to do — develop a strategy to gather and manage the information you need. You could try to remember and count every card as they are played, but doing so will almost inevitably lead to errors. Most cards are irrelevant — the trick is to work out, in advance, which ones are not. Throughout this book we concentrate on how to develop a useful IMS. The essential ingredient of sound declarer play (and defense) is to recognize the problem; you then adjust your line of play and counting strategy to provide the information needed to solve it.

On this hand, the first step is to make sure you can ruff your club loser safely in dummy. You have nine trumps, leaving four for the defenders. As long as the trumps are not 4-0, you can afford to draw all of the defenders' trumps before playing clubs. What other information do you need to keep track of?

One of your chances for a thirteenth trick is dummy's long diamond. It would be pointless to get to trick twelve and then not know if the last diamond is a winner. If the diamond is not good at trick twelve, then you will have to take the spade finesse and hope, so your counting strategy is to make sure trumps break and to count diamonds. Nothing else.

Having come to this conclusion, it's time to play. East follows with a heart at trick one, so you know trumps are not 4-0 and thus your first problem is solved. You draw as many trumps as are necessary (by watching to see whether the suit breaks 2-2 or 3-1) and then you play three rounds of clubs, ruffing in dummy. While you have been playing these first few tricks, you should have been paying attention to one thing and one thing only — has either defender thrown a diamond? Assuming the answer is no, then you know there are still six outstanding. If dummy's long diamond is to be a winner, then you will need the suit to break 3-3. You cash the three top diamonds ending in dummy. If both defenders follow to three rounds of diamonds, you know that dummy's last diamond is good, and you are home free. If either defender discards on any of these tricks, then diamonds were not 3-3 and you take the spade finesse.

Notice that, before playing to trick one, you knew exactly which cards to focus your attention on. It is possible that your initial IMS will suggest you need to watch cards in two suits, but this can be an illusion as the next hand illustrates:

```
Both Vul.          ♠   8 5 3
Lead: ♠4           ♥   K 6
                   ♦   A Q 7 3
                   ♣   Q 6 4 2

              ┌──────────────┐
              │       N      │
              │  W        E  │
              │       S      │
              └──────────────┘

                   ♠   Q 7 2
                   ♥   A 7
                   ♦   K 9 5 4
                   ♣   A K 8 3
```

WEST	NORTH	EAST	SOUTH
		pass	1NT
pass	3NT	all pass	

East wins the spade lead with the king and returns the ♠9. You cover and West takes the ace, cashes the jack (East following), and leads the thirteenth spade. Fortunately, the defenders haven't beaten your contract off the top, so it is time to count tricks and develop your IMS. You have eight top tricks — two hearts, three diamonds and three clubs. Your ninth trick can come from a 3-2 break in either minor. In order to ensure that you will make your contract whichever suit breaks, on the fourth spade you discard a diamond from one hand and a club from the other.

It looks as if you have to keep track of the five outstanding cards in both minor suits. While this is not a particularly arduous task on this hand, it is nonetheless unnecessary. Let's say you ignore diamonds and concentrate on the five missing clubs. East throws a red card on the fourth round of spades and West plays a heart. You win and cash the top clubs, paying attention to whether the suit breaks. If both defenders follow to two rounds of clubs, you are home. If someone discards, then you will have to hope diamonds break. You do not need to count diamonds at all. You plan to cash your winners and lead your last diamond at Trick 13 — you'll find out then whether it's good or not! Of course, you could equally well have concentrated on counting the diamonds and ignored the clubs, in which case you would have cashed the top diamonds first.

On the next hand it seems at first that you must keep track of three suits, but this, too, is a mirage:

Neither Vul.   ♠ 8 4 2
Lead: ♥Q   ♥ K 5 4
                ♦ K Q 7
                ♣ A 8 6 2

```
        N
    W       E
        S
```

♠ A K Q 3
♥ A 7
♦ A 6 4 3
♣ K 7 4

WEST	NORTH	EAST	SOUTH
			2NT
pass	6 NT	all pass	

You have ten top tricks, with obvious chances in three suits; you need two of those three suits to divide 3-3 to make twelve tricks. If both diamonds and spades break, you will be home no matter what you do. However, you also want to be able to score an extra club if you need it. Clearly, you cannot play ace, king and a third club, because if clubs are 4-2 the defense will take two club tricks. Nor can you cash your spade and diamond winners before giving up a club, as the defense may be able to cash a second winner when they get their club trick.

The answer is to win the ♥Q lead and play a low club from each hand. East wins and plays a second heart. Now you cash all of your winners while counting so that you know which long cards are good. It doesn't matter which suit you cash first, but it is easiest to start with clubs, as you have already played one round. There are six cards outstanding in both diamonds and spades, and four in clubs. For a long card in a suit to become good, you need an even split.

Let's say that when you cash the ♣AK everyone follows, so the four missing clubs have broken 2-2 and dummy's thirteenth club is good. It is tempting to cash it now, but stop! Which of your potential winners are you going to discard on it — the thirteenth spade or the thirteenth diamond? No — much better to leave the club winner in dummy for now.

You will need an entry to dummy to score the long club later, so leave the diamonds intact and start on spades next. Note that you are now in the same position as you were on the last hand. There are two suits to count, diamonds and spades, but you only need to concentrate on one of them — spades, since that is the suit you intend to test first.

There are six spades missing, so you need them to break 3-3. Before you play any spades, fix in your mind that you need both defenders to follow to all three spade winners. If they do, you have twelve tricks. You will take your long spade, cross to dummy in diamonds, cash the long club, and return to the other top diamonds. If someone discards on a top spade, you cross to the ♦K, cash the thirteenth club throwing your spade loser, and hope diamonds break 3-3. There is no need even to count the diamonds. Either they break and your thirteenth diamond is good, or they don't and the contract fails.

Let us now go back to the point at which you cashed the ♣AK and say that a defender discards on the third round. Now you need both spades and diamonds to break 3-3. Since the missing spades and diamonds are both still relevant, you must pay attention to the discard on the third round of clubs. If the discard is a heart then you cash the spades as you did above, knowing that you need both defenders to follow three times. But what if someone discards a spade on the third club? As there are now only five spades out, you cash the top spades watching to make sure both defenders follow twice.

Readers who know something about squeezes will know that the order in which you cash your winners can sometimes be important. On the next hand, we shall see how developing a sound IMS allows you to capitalize when an opponent 'throws the wrong card.' Effectively, this will help you to execute a simple squeeze without needing to plan it, or even to know that it is happening!

Neither Vul.
Lead: ♣10

♠ 6 5
♥ 6 4 3
♦ A K Q 10 2
♣ A 7 6

♠ A J
♥ A K Q J
♦ 8 7 5
♣ K Q J 5

WEST	NORTH	EAST	SOUTH
			2NT
pass	3♦	pass	4♦
pass	4NT	pass	5♥
pass	7NT	all pass	

You see twelve top tricks and if diamonds break, you can claim. Even if diamonds are 4-1, as long as West has ♦Jxxx you will be able to score the ♦10 via a marked finesse. You take East's ♠Q with the ace and cash the ♦AK, but West discards a spade on the second diamond. Now you cannot score a fourth diamond trick without first losing to East's jack. Is there anything you can do?

Actually, yes, and it involves a squeeze. But you don't need to know anything about squeezes except that, if you cash winners, a defender sometimes throws something helpful. Which cards are relevant? There is only one — the ♠K. If anyone throws that card away you will be able to score the ♠J. So, cash your winners and see what happens — does the ♠K appear?

```
              ♠  6 5
              ♥  6 4 3
              ♦  A K Q 10 2
              ♣  A 7 6
```

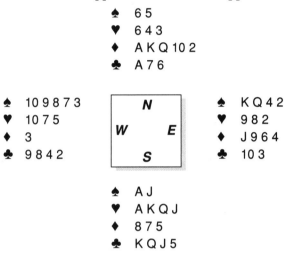

```
♠  10 9 8 7 3                    ♠  K Q 4 2
♥  10 7 5                        ♥  9 8 2
♦  3                             ♦  J 9 6 4
♣  9 8 4 2                       ♣  10 3
```

```
              ♠  A J
              ♥  A K Q J
              ♦  8 7 5
              ♣  K Q J 5
```

After you have taken a spade, two diamonds, four clubs and three hearts, these cards remain:

```
              ♠  —
              ♥  —
              ♦  Q 10 2
              ♣  —
```

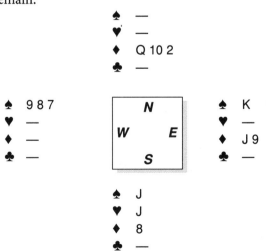

```
♠  9 8 7                         ♠  K
♥  —                             ♥  —
♦  —                             ♦  J 9
♣  —                             ♣  —
```

```
              ♠  J
              ♥  J
              ♦  8
              ♣  —
```

When you cash your last heart winner, East will be forced to discard either a diamond or the ♠K. You decided earlier what to do if the ♠K was discarded — cash the jack. If the ♠K hasn't appeared, then you will just have to hope the diamonds are good after all.

So what happened? You had all of the remaining tricks except one and East was genuinely squeezed because in the two-card ending he needed to keep three cards. You did not have to plan in advance that this was going to happen, you just had to know what to look for so you could take advantage if it did.

Managing the available information and knowing what to do with it is vital on many hands. This, coupled with sound technique, sees declarer home on the final hand in this chapter:

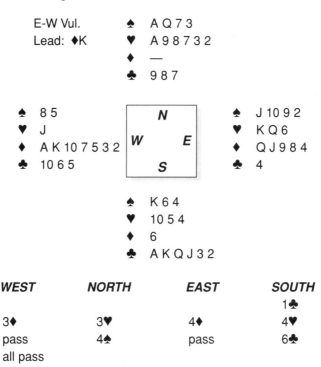

E-W Vul.
Lead: ♦K

North:
♠ A Q 7 3
♥ A 9 8 7 3 2
♦ —
♣ 9 8 7

West:
♠ 8 5
♥ J
♦ A K 10 7 5 3 2
♣ 10 6 5

East:
♠ J 10 9 2
♥ K Q 6
♦ Q J 9 8 4
♣ 4

South:
♠ K 6 4
♥ 10 5 4
♦ 6
♣ A K Q J 3 2

WEST	NORTH	EAST	SOUTH
			1♣
3♦	3♥	4♦	4♥
pass	4♠	pass	6♣
all pass			

At first glance, the contract seems to depend on one of the major suits dividing evenly. You ruff the diamond lead, draw trumps, and duck a heart. East overtakes West's ♥J with the king and returns the ♠J to dummy's queen. You cash the ♥A, knowing that if everyone follows, the suit was originally 2-2 and you are home. West discards a diamond. You have one chance left — spades may break 3-3 so you...

Stop! Unless you have a train to catch, what's the rush to find out if spades break? As we saw on the last hand, when you have all but one of the remaining tricks it is usually right to cash your winners and see what happens. You don't need to envision the ending or work out what either defender has. All you must know is what to look for. You do not even need to keep track of two suits. There is only one card you are looking for — the ♥Q. If it is discarded you know to cash the ♥10. If not, then you will have to hope spades break.

So you cross back to hand with the ♠K and cash two more trumps. These are the last three cards:

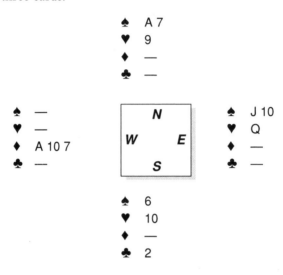

As it happens, when you cash your last club (throwing dummy's heart) East has a choice of losing discards — the ♥Q or a spade. One benefit of developing an IMS is that when something unexpected like a squeeze occurs, you are ready to take advantage of it.

There are many types of counting skills in bridge, and you will rarely play a hand on which you do not need at least one of them. In this chapter, we have seen how to keep track of cards efficiently. Using the information you gain by counting to build a picture of the closed hands, both in terms of high cards and of distribution, will help you solve many problems. Examples of how to do this are given throughout this book.

To get started, practice by concentrating on one of the unseen hands only. Once you have a complete count of one defender's shape or high cards, always work out what that leaves the other closed hand. This not only cross-checks your arithmetic, but enables you to see solutions and/or problems from two different perspectives.

However, knowing what each defender has will do you no good at all on many hands. So, how do you know when you need to count the defenders' hands? How often have you reached Trick 9 and thought, 'Is the ♦6 good? If only I had counted the diamonds on this hand.' Deciding which cards are relevant at the outset by developing an accurate IMS will solve most problems of this nature. However, there is a safety valve if you miss something in your initial analysis.

If we return to our example of the brain as a fuel tank, you will realize that you will quickly exhaust your mental energy if you religiously count the opponents' hands on every deal. So, how do you know which hands you need to count? The simple answer is that you don't. You must therefore train your subconscious mind to count for you. When you are driving a car, why do you get tired more quickly when it is dark and raining than when it is clear and dry? The answer is that when the weather is poor you have to concentrate harder — it is a strain to see and you must be more aware of stopping distances, and so forth. You know that you must actively pay attention. On a bright and sunny day you do exactly the same things — watch the road and calculate distances and speeds — but you do these things easily and automatically. They are a habit. Under normal conditions, your mind is trained to do all the necessary things without conscious thought.

Similarly, you must train your mind to follow what is happening at the bridge table without having to make an active effort to do so. Then, when you get to Trick 9, if you need to know whether the ♦6 is good (but didn't realize it when you devised your initial plan) you can mentally replay the first eight tricks and come up with the correct answer. As a result, on those hands where you have no need to count the defenders' hands, you won't have wasted your mental energy doing so.

Training your mind to do this is simpler than you might think. Next time you play in a relaxed game — one where you are not under pressure to play quickly — make a serious effort to count the opponents' hands on every deal. You will find it hard work, and for a while you'll probably play worse as you concentrate on counting. However, after you have done this for just two or three sessions, you will find that you are no longer actively thinking about counting, but that, if you need the information, it is there.

At first, you may find you cannot keep track of enough information to count a complete hand. Since knowing the distribution of two suits puts you most of the way there, practice by keeping track of just two suits. Once you are comfortable with that, add a third suit. Remember to start by counting only one of the unseen hands, though.

Eventually, you will come to realize that counting at bridge need not even be as difficult as counting to thirteen. Throughout the rest of this book we shall outline numerous situations in which you can use your new-found skills to improve your results significantly.

- Identify which suits are important (i.e. where your extra tricks can come from).

- Decide which suits you must count or which high cards to watch for.

- Fix in your mind how many cards are outstanding in each of the key suits.

- Count by keeping track of *missing* cards.

- Think in terms of how the missing cards might break rather than the total number of outstanding cards.

- Count only *one* of the unseen hands.

- Once you know the shape of one unseen hand, work out the distribution of the other.

CHAPTER 3

Clues from the Bidding

In the early days of bridge, you were supposed to have a decent hand to open, and even more so to compete once the opponents had opened the bidding. Everything revolved around avoiding unnecessary penalties. In the modern game, the philosophy is almost exactly the opposite. Players take great risks to get in a bid that will direct the lead, or might simply disrupt their opponents' auction. This kind of approach can be a double-edged sword, however: competitive auctions often provide the eventual declarer with critical information. Sometimes, the bidding warns him of bad breaks; on other occasions it locates the defenders' high cards. Our first hand illustrates how an innocent opening bid can make life easier for declarer:

Neither Vul.
Lead: ♠6

	♠	J 8 5 3
	♥	A 9 3
	♦	A 7 6
	♣	J 7 2

```
        N
    W       E
        S
```

	♠	K Q 10 9 4
	♥	Q 7
	♦	K 10 4
	♣	A K 5

WEST	NORTH	EAST	SOUTH
			1♠
pass	3♠	pass	4♠
all pass			

Despite a combined 27 HCP and a 5-4 trump fit, when you count your tricks there are only nine. You have a certain spade lose and, probably one in diamonds (barring ♦QJ doubleton), as well as potential losers in the other two suits. It seems you will need either the ♥K onside or the ♣Q to drop doubleton. Now consider the same hand with East as the dealer:

WEST	NORTH	EAST	SOUTH
		1♥	1♠
pass	2♥	pass	4♠
all pass			

Now your contract is virtually assured, since East surely has the ♥K. The defense starts with a trump to the ace and another trump, everyone following, so you win in dummy and lead a heart towards the queen. Whether East rises with the king or not, your contract is secure.

Now let's make West the dealer.

WEST	NORTH	EAST	SOUTH
1♥	pass	pass	dbl
pass	2♥	pass	3♠
pass	4♠	all pass	

Suppose West leads ace and another trump. This time you can expect at least twelve of the missing high-card points to be on your left. One line of play to take advantage of this information is to win the second trump in dummy and lead a diamond to the ten (to keep East off lead if he has the jack). Let's say West wins and exits safely with a diamond. It is now a simple matter to cash your diamond winners and play three rounds of clubs. Unless the ♣Q drops (in which case you have ten tricks), West will be forced to win the third round. He will then have to concede your tenth trick, either by leading a heart away from his king or by giving you a ruff-and-discard in a minor suit.

Opening the bidding with twelve or thirteen high card points is quite normal, but doing so in the two auctions above pinpointed the defenders' high cards. All that was left was for you to make use of that information. Making the most of all the available information is the theme of our second hand, which was originally presented as a BOLS Bridge Tip by the legendary Bobby Wolff. The lesson is well worth repeating.

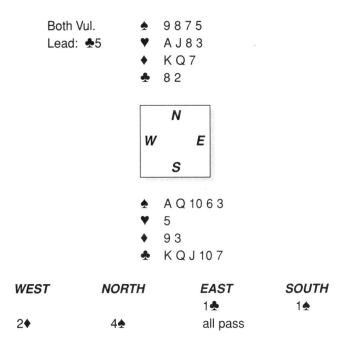

Both Vul.
Lead: ♣5

♠	9 8 7 5
♥	A J 8 3
♦	K Q 7
♣	8 2

♠	A Q 10 6 3
♥	5
♦	9 3
♣	K Q J 10 7

WEST	NORTH	EAST	SOUTH
		1♣	1♠
2♦	4♠	all pass	

The hand occurred in a team-of-four match. The auction and play were identical at both tables but one declarer based his actions on flimsy reasoning while the other backed a certain winner.

East wins the ♣A, returns a diamond to West's ace, and ruffs the second round of diamonds with the ♠2. East then exits with a club on which West plays the ♣4. Clearly you cannot afford a trump loser, so you cross to dummy's ♥A and lead the ♠9. What do you do when East follows with the ♠4 and, more importantly, why? As a hint, ask yourself what information you can glean not only from what an opponent did, but also from what he did not do.

In the match, both declarers ran the ♠9 and, when West discarded on the trick, they repeated the trump finesse to score up their game. One declarer commented that West had already shown up with five points in diamonds so it was likely that East had both spade honors for his opening bid. Is this a sufficiently good reason for taking the double spade finesse? Even without the ♠J, East would have twelve points and a singleton — surely enough for an opening bid.

Why did the second declarer also play West for a spade void? The answer is obvious if you think about what East did *not* do — he did not open 1♥. He opened 1♣ on a four-card suit, and he also had a singleton diamond. Since he would not open 1♣ with only four clubs holding a five-card major, East must be exactly 4-4-1-4. West therefore had no spades.

Wolff's BOLS Tip was, *'Do not be content simply to work out the high cards a defender is likely to have for the bids he made. Also try to picture his distribution, for this may provide an even surer guide to the winning play.'*

In our next example, West has an opening bid including eleven black cards. Most of us would bid as this West did, but notice how much easier the play becomes when declarer is armed with a blueprint of the distribution:

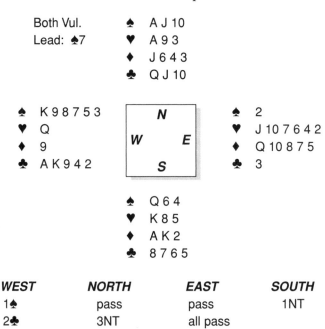

Both Vul.
Lead: ♠7

	♠	A J 10
	♥	A 9 3
	♦	J 6 4 3
	♣	Q J 10

♠ K 9 8 7 5 3	♠ 2
♥ Q	♥ J 10 7 6 4 2
♦ 9	♦ Q 10 8 7 5
♣ A K 9 4 2	♣ 3

	♠	Q 6 4
	♥	K 8 5
	♦	A K 2
	♣	8 7 6 5

WEST	NORTH	EAST	SOUTH
1♠	pass	pass	1NT
2♣	3NT	all pass	

Look at just the North-South cards. Had North been the dealer, the bidding might easily have been 1♦-(Pass)-3NT — not nearly so helpful as the actual auction. With West bidding twice opposite a passing partner, you can immediately place him with at least ten black-suit cards. When a defender has only three unknown cards at the outset, it is fairly easy to determine his exact distribution at an early stage. You can also place most of the outstanding high cards with the opener.

The ♠7 is led, and dummy's ♠10 holds trick one. You can count seven tricks (three spades with the aid of the finesse and four top red-suit winners). As an eighth trick can be built in clubs by force, you lead that suit at trick two. West takes the ♣K and exits with a spade to dummy's jack. East discards a heart and you make a mental note that spades were 6-1. Pursuing the aim of developing a club trick, you continue the suit. East's diamond discard is no surprise and confirms eleven of West's cards. West wins the ♣A and returns the suit as East throws a second diamond. You cash the ♦K and West follows. When he also follows to the ♥K, his original distribution is revealed as 6-1-1-5 (and East's as 1-6-5-1). The position is now:

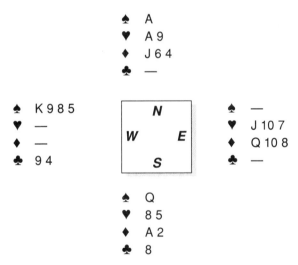

```
                   ♠  A
                   ♥  A 9
                   ♦  J 6 4
                   ♣  —

   ♠  K 9 8 5          N          ♠  —
   ♥  —                           ♥  J 10 7
   ♦  —          W          E     ♦  Q 10 8
   ♣  9 4               S         ♣  —

                   ♠  Q
                   ♥  8 5
                   ♦  A 2
                   ♣  8
```

You still need to generate an extra trick. The ♦J seems to be your only prospect but you might wonder how that card can ever be a winner given East's holding in the suit. You have a complete count of the hand, so a new perspective might offer some clues. Move around the table and put yourself in East's seat for a moment. If the ♠A is cashed, what do you suppose he will discard?

If East discards a heart, then you will be able to cash the ♥A and exit with a heart to leave him on play — with only diamonds left, he will have to lead away from the ♦Q. If, instead, he discards a diamond, then two rounds of that suit will establish dummy's long diamond while the ♥A remains as an entry. Either way, the ♦J will be your ninth trick.

Now that you have the idea, it's time to test your counting skill as declarer:

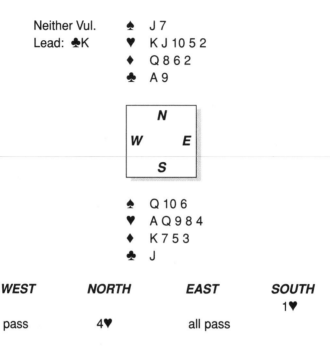

Neither Vul.
Lead: ♣K

♠ J 7
♥ K J 10 5 2
♦ Q 8 6 2
♣ A 9

♠ Q 10 6
♥ A Q 9 8 4
♦ K 7 5 3
♣ J

WEST	NORTH	EAST	SOUTH
			1♥
pass	4♥	all pass	

You cannot avoid losing two spade tricks and the ♦A, so you must avoid a second diamond loser. To achieve this goal, you will have to find a defender with the ♦A singleton or doubleton, and you will have to 'guess' whether that person is East or West.

You start by winning the ♣A and drawing trumps, noting West's club discard on the second round. When you lead the ♠J from dummy, West wins the ♠K and tries to cash a club, which you ruff. East wins the second round of spades with the ace and exits safely with a third spade. You are at the crossroads. Which defender do you play for the ♦A?

West has shown up with eight points in the black suits plus a singleton heart. If he has a doubleton ♦A his hand will look something like:

♠ K x x x		♠ K x x x x
♥ x	*or*	♥ x
♦ A x		♦ A x
♣ K Q x x x x		♣ K Q x x x

With either of these hands, West surely would have bid over your 1♥ opening. You should therefore play East for the doubleton ♦A. You cross to dummy with a trump and lead a diamond to your king. If that wins, hold your breath and duck the second round of diamonds to what you hope is East's now bare ace. The full hand is:

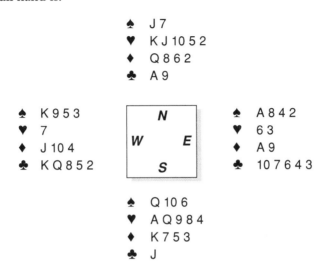

                 ♠ J 7
                 ♥ K J 10 5 2
                 ♦ Q 8 6 2
                 ♣ A 9

♠ K 9 5 3		♠ A 8 4 2
♥ 7	**N**	♥ 6 3
♦ J 10 4	**W** **E**	♦ A 9
♣ K Q 8 5 2	**S**	♣ 10 7 6 4 3

                 ♠ Q 10 6
                 ♥ A Q 9 8 4
                 ♦ K 7 5 3
                 ♣ J

Often, you will need to combine a number of factors to help you make the winning choice from among the various options. Clues from an opponent's bidding, or lack of it, are an integral part of the jigsaw puzzle. You may have to base your play on how you decide a particular suit is breaking, or on which defender you think holds a key honor card. Counting will often provide the information you need to reach the correct conclusion. Drawing inferences from the bidding is a theme we shall return to continually.

When the opponents get into your auction, sometimes they prevent you from reaching your best contract or are able to find a profitable sacrifice. They have won those battles. To balance the ledger, you must extract full price from the information provided by their bidding when you do become declarer.

- **Always** remember the bidding.

- Take note of what an opponent's bids show.

- Take note when an opponent *fails* to bid, and use this information to help you place high cards and figure out the distribution.

- When a defender shows a distributional hand in the bidding, concentrate on discovering his exact shape early.

- Once you can 'see' a defender's hand, mentally move around the table and consider the play from his perspective.

CHAPTER 4

Counting the Defenders' High Card Points

hether you learned bridge by attending classes, reading books, or just by playing, the first card play technique you mastered was almost certainly the finesse. Long-suffering teachers know it often takes considerable effort to talk a beginner into taking that first finesse. Once over the initial hurdle though, most players quickly find the lure of a cheap trick too addictive for their own good.

You have probably noticed that good players seem to have an uncanny knack of avoiding finesses that are destined to lose. However, this is not a skill that only champions can acquire. One reason for taking what may appear to be a wildly anti-percentage line of play is that you know the normal-looking finesse will fail. Here is a straightforward example that everyone should get right at the table but which, in practice, few would. Cover the defenders' hands if you feel like testing yourself.

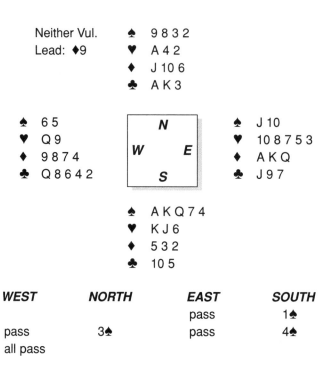

	Neither Vul. Lead: ♦9	♠ 9 8 3 2 ♥ A 4 2 ♦ J 10 6 ♣ A K 3	

```
          ♠  9 8 3 2
          ♥  A 4 2
          ♦  J 10 6
          ♣  A K 3

♠  6 5                    ♠  J 10
♥  Q 9          N         ♥  10 8 7 5 3
♦  9 8 7 4   W     E      ♦  A K Q
♣  Q 8 6 4 2    S         ♣  J 9 7

          ♠  A K Q 7 4
          ♥  K J 6
          ♦  5 3 2
          ♣  10 5
```

WEST	NORTH	EAST	SOUTH
		pass	1♠
pass	3♠	pass	4♠
all pass			

Poor distribution makes dummy a disappointment despite its twelve high card points. At first sight, it seems that the contract will depend on the heart finesse at best. You cover the opening diamond lead with dummy's ten. East wins with the queen, cashes the ♦AK, and switches to the ♠J. Both defenders follow to two rounds of trumps, and adhering to the sound practice of delaying the decision in the crucial suit, you play three rounds of clubs, ruffing in hand as East follows with the jack.

Now it's decision time.

Everyone knows the correct way to play this heart suit for three tricks — cash the ace and finesse the jack on the way back. However, since you have been listening and counting, you decide to ignore the odds and cash the hearts from the top. Your alertness is rewarded when the ♥Q falls doubleton on your left. Of course, you were lucky to find a doubleton queen with seven hearts missing, but to finesse against East would have been giving up. The reason is surprisingly obvious if you think about the bidding. East had shown up with the ♦AKQ and two black-suit jacks — eleven points — yet he passed as dealer. Was it really possible that he would also have the ♥Q?

Counting the defenders' points and recalling their bidding, or lack thereof, may allow you to make contracts in spectacular fashion. With that clue, try this problem:

N-S Vul. ♠ A Q 8 5
Lead: ♥K ♥ 7 5 2
     ♦ 6
     ♣ K Q 9 5 3

```
        N
    W       E
        S
```

     ♠ J 10 9 6 2
     ♥ 9 6 3
     ♦ A K Q 10 8
     ♣ —

WEST	NORTH	EAST	SOUTH
		pass	pass
pass	1♣	pass	1♠
pass	2♠	pass	4♠
all pass			

West leads the king, queen and jack of hearts. East overtakes the third round and returns a diamond. Do you have a plan?

A non-counting declarer would win the ♦A and run the ♠J without much pause for thought. Can you find a valid reason for doing anything other than just taking a trump finesse? In earlier chapters we have tried to emphasize the importance of finding out as much as possible about the hand before making the critical decision. Can you see a way to obtain more information here?

If you cannot think of anything, try the effect of ruffing a diamond in dummy and leading the ♣K (this is technically known as a 'discovery play'). If East follows with a small club, will it not be clear that West holds the ♣A? Once you decide that West has the ♣A, what conclusion do you draw concerning the position of the ♠K? This is the full hand:

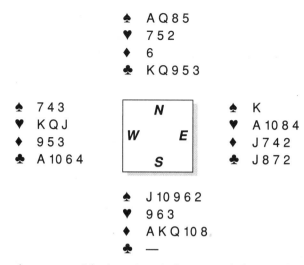

♠ A Q 8 5
♥ 7 5 2
♦ 6
♣ K Q 9 5 3

♠ 7 4 3   ♠ K
♥ K Q J   ♥ A 10 8 4
♦ 9 5 3   ♦ J 7 4 2
♣ A 10 6 4   ♣ J 8 7 2

♠ J 10 9 6 2
♥ 9 6 3
♦ A K Q 10 8
♣ —

West has shown up with six points in hearts and the ♣A (by inference), yet he failed to open. He cannot have the ♠K, so your only hope is that it is single-ton! Play a spade to the ace and accept the kibitzers' applause. Most declarers would finesse, go down, shrug, and go on to the next hand, never realizing they should have done the right thing. It may seem like a spectacular 'expert' play, but if you make the effort to count the defenders' points, it is not so difficult.

Similar inferences exist when a player fails to respond to an opening bid:

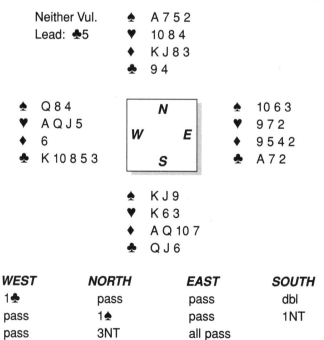

Neither Vul.   ♠ A 7 5 2
Lead: ♣5   ♥ 10 8 4
                ♦ K J 8 3
                ♣ 9 4

♠ Q 8 4   ♠ 10 6 3
♥ A Q J 5   ♥ 9 7 2
♦ 6   ♦ 9 5 4 2
♣ K 10 8 5 3   ♣ A 7 2

♠ K J 9
♥ K 6 3
♦ A Q 10 7
♣ Q J 6

WEST	NORTH	EAST	SOUTH
1♣	pass	pass	dbl
pass	1♠	pass	1NT
pass	3NT	all pass	

West leads the ♣5 to his partner's ace. East returns the ♣7, and West takes his king and clears the suit as East follows with the ♣2.

You can count seven top tricks — four diamonds, one club and two spades. Clearly your two extra tricks will have to come from spades. The normal way to play this suit for four tricks is to finesse East for the queen, but his bidding (or lack of it) is revealing. Since he failed to respond to his partner's 1♣ opening and has shown up with the ♣A (too much for many players already!), there is no realistic chance that he will also have the ♠Q.

How can you make four spade tricks when West holds the ♠Q over your jack? Try leading the ♠J. West covers and you win the ace. Do you see what has happened? This 'backwards finesse' against the ♠Q has created a normal finesse position against the ♠10. When the finesse of the ♠9 wins and the suit breaks 3-3 you have nine tricks — one club, four diamonds and four spades. You have made another 'impossible' contract. How did you do it? Simply by counting to six — the number of points on which most players respond to their partner's opening bid.

Passing can be most informative if it limits the defender to a narrow range of high card points. The same is true of well-defined bids, particularly a 1NT opening.

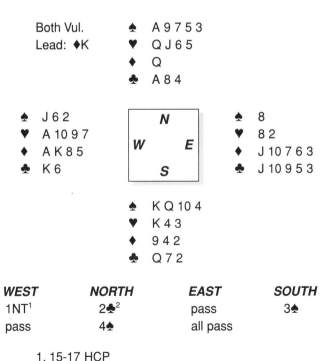

Both Vul.
Lead: ♦K

	♠	A 9 7 5 3
	♥	Q J 6 5
	♦	Q
	♣	A 8 4

West:
♠	J 6 2
♥	A 10 9 7
♦	A K 8 5
♣	K 6

East:
♠	8
♥	8 2
♦	J 10 7 6 3
♣	J 10 9 5 3

South:
♠	K Q 10 4
♥	K 4 3
♦	9 4 2
♣	Q 7 2

WEST	NORTH	EAST	SOUTH
1NT[1]	2♣[2]	pass	3♠
pass	4♠	all pass	

1. 15-17 HCP
2. Majors

West leads the ♦K and switches to a trump. Taking East's ♠8 in hand with the ten, you lead a heart to dummy's queen, which wins. You cash the ♠AK, West following while East pitches once from each minor. You lead a second small heart from hand (in case West started with a doubleton ace) and dummy's jack wins. On the third round of hearts, your king loses to West as East throws another diamond. West exits with the fourth round of hearts, which you ruff.

What do you know so far? West has shown up with the ♠J, the ♥A and, based on the opening lead, the ♦AK. Even if he has both missing jacks, that is still only fourteen points. Surely, he must have the ♣K, so playing a club to the queen does not look promising. Only one option remains — you play a club to the ace and duck the second round of clubs. Lo and behold, West's king comes down doubleton and you claim your contract. Yes, you were lucky to find the ♣K dropping, but don't you think you deserved your good fortune?

The situation appears to be similar on the next hand, but is it?

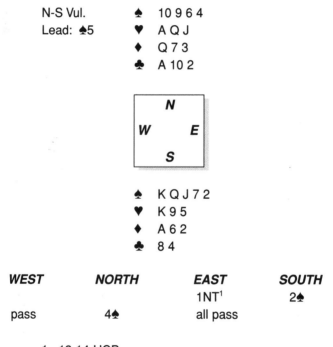

N-S Vul.
Lead: ♠5

♠ 10 9 6 4
♥ A Q J
♦ Q 7 3
♣ A 10 2

```
        N
    W       E
        S
```

♠ K Q J 7 2
♥ K 9 5
♦ A 6 2
♣ 8 4

WEST	NORTH	EAST	SOUTH
		1NT¹	2♠
pass	4♠	all pass	

1. 12-14 HCP

East wins the trump lead with the ace and switches to the ♣K. You duck, win the ♣Q continuation with your ace, and draw a second round of trumps to which both defenders follow. You can count nine tricks, but prospects seem bleak since East must have the ♦K over dummy's queen to make up his opening bid. On the previous hand, you had to resort to dropping the doubleton king when you needed two tricks from Axx opposite Qxx. Are you in the same position again?

A count of the distribution confirms that the chances of finding East with the ♦Kx are remote, since he is already known to hold a doubleton spade. He could be 2-4-2-5, but most players prefer to open 1♣, not 1NT, with that shape. There is an alternative line of play available though — one which requires only that East holds the ♣J, which seems likely based on the early play.

You cash three rounds of hearts ending in dummy and lead the ♣10. East covers with the jack as expected, and you discard a diamond. What can East do? If he leads a club or a heart, you ruff in dummy and throw your second diamond loser. If he leads a diamond, you run it to dummy's queen. Either way, you come to ten tricks. This is the full hand:

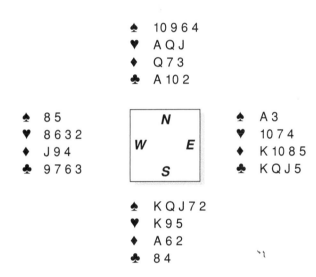

```
                    ♠  10 9 6 4
                    ♥  A Q J
                    ♦  Q 7 3
                    ♣  A 10 2

  ♠  8 5              N           ♠  A 3
  ♥  8 6 3 2                      ♥  10 7 4
  ♦  J 9 4       W       E        ♦  K 10 8 5
  ♣  9 7 6 3          S           ♣  K Q J 5

                    ♠  K Q J 7 2
                    ♥  K 9 5
                    ♦  A 6 2
                    ♣  8 4
```

You always had to lose one diamond trick. This 'loser-on-loser' play simply swaps that diamond loser for a club loser. In so doing, you were able to end-play East at the same time.

On the hands so far, you have counted points as the defenders' played their high cards. You have also inferred which defender held a specific card from the early play or the bidding. Sometimes you must actually place a card in one defender's hand because, if he doesn't have it, the contract cannot be made. Here is an example of this kind of counting:

Neither Vul.
Lead: ♠A

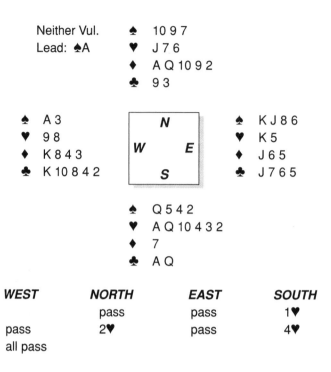

```
                    ♠  10 9 7
                    ♥  J 7 6
                    ♦  A Q 10 9 2
                    ♣  9 3

  ♠  A 3                            ♠  K J 8 6
  ♥  9 8              N             ♥  K 5
  ♦  K 8 4 3      W       E         ♦  J 6 5
  ♣  K 10 8 4 2       S             ♣  J 7 6 5

                    ♠  Q 5 4 2
                    ♥  A Q 10 4 3 2
                    ♦  7
                    ♣  A Q
```

WEST	NORTH	EAST	SOUTH
	pass	pass	1♥
pass	2♥	pass	4♥
all pass			

West kicks off with the ♠A and a second spade to East's king. East returns the ♠J, you cover with the queen, and West ruffs. Now he exits with the ♦8.

Looking at all four hands, it is easy to see that you should take the diamond finesse. When that wins you will be able to draw trumps, ruff your spade loser, and discard the ♣Q on the ♦A. How could you figure out to play the hand in this manner, though? You have three losers to worry about — a trump, a spade and a club. As you cannot afford to lose another trick, you must assume East has the ♥K, which will allow you to ruff your last spade in dummy (with the jack if necessary). That's two potential losers dealt with. All that remains is to decide which minor-suit finesse to take. This appears to be a guess, but is it?

East has shown up with the ♠KJ and you have given him the ♥K too (on the basis that you cannot make the contract if West has that card). If the club finesse is winning, who has the ♦K? You will recall that East failed to open the bidding. If he has the ♠KJ, the ♥K and the ♣K, then he cannot also have the ♦K. This means that if the club finesse works, so will the diamond finesse. However, West *can* hold both minor-suit kings (as he does in the diagram) and so it is right to finesse the diamond. Of course, if East has the ♦K you will go down, but if that happens you never had any chance since either the heart or club finesse is also bound to lose.

N-S Vul.
Lead: ♥J

♠	K 10 8 3
♥	A Q 6
♦	9 2
♣	8 6 5 2

♠	A J 9 6 2
♥	8 3
♦	J 10 5
♣	K Q 3

WEST	NORTH	EAST	SOUTH
pass	pass	pass	1♠
pass	3♠	pass	4♠
all pass			

Your raise to game was obviously based on something other than the hand you have, and now your play must justify your bidding. You try the ♥Q at trick one and it holds. How do you play the spades?

As usual, you should delay the decision until you know more about the hand. You lead a diamond at trick two, East winning the king and returning a second heart to the ace. When you lead dummy's second diamond, East takes the ace and exits with a third heart which you ruff. Have you made a decision about the spades yet?

It's time to count the defenders' points. East has shown up with the ♦AK and you need him to have the ♣A. However, he did not open the bidding and so you should play the ♠A and a spade to the ten. If East wins the queen then you were going down anyway, since the ♣A must be over your king. This could be the full hand:

```
              ♠  K 10 8 3
              ♥  A Q 6
              ♦  9 2
              ♣  8 6 5 2

   ♠  Q 5 4        ┌─────────┐        ♠  7
   ♥  K J 10 9     │    N    │        ♥  7 5 4 2
   ♦  Q 8 6 3      │ W     E │        ♦  A K 7 4
   ♣  J 9          │    S    │        ♣  A 10 7 4
                   └─────────┘
              ♠  A J 9 6 2
              ♥  8 3
              ♦  J 10 5
              ♣  K Q 3
```

Finally, let's say that instead of raising yourself to game you sensibly passed 3♠. The defense starts the same way (three rounds of diamonds) and again you must decide how to play trumps. Does a count of the defenders' points suggest you should play differently because you are a level lower?

Clearly, if East has the ♣A then you can always make nine tricks by drawing trumps and leading twice towards the ♣KQ. Therefore, the contract is only in danger if West has the ♣A and you lose a trick to the ♠Q. What has West shown up with? You can place him with the ♥KJ and the ♦Q (unless East is playing a very deep game). If he also has the ♣A, then he cannot have the ♠Q having passed as dealer. You should therefore play a spade to the king and lead the ♠10. If East follows small, run the ten. If the spade finesse loses, you can be sure the ♣A is onside and that you will still make nine tricks. If West discards on the second round of spades, you can draw the last trump and concede two clubs. Either way, you will fulfill your contract.

- **Remember the bidding.** As defenders play honor cards, think about how many points their bidding (or lack of bidding) showed.

- Count the points of a defender who has shown a limited hand.

- If a defender has limited his hand in the bidding, do not play him for an honor he *cannot* have, even if it means taking an anti-percentage play in the suit.

- If you need a defender to have a specific card, assume he has that card and base your play on that assumption.

Counting as Declarer

CHAPTER 5

Concentrating on the Distribution

In the last chapter we limited ourselves to counting high card points. The second aspect of counting is the cornerstone of sound declarer play — determining the shape of the defenders' hands. This task is simplified when an opponent has made a descriptive bid. To illustrate, we start with some deals on which a defender shows a two-suited hand. At trick one you already know ten of his cards — a little discovery enables you to identify the remaining three cards, thereby completing the distributional count. When you can effectively 'see' the defenders' hands like this, it significantly improves your chances as declarer.

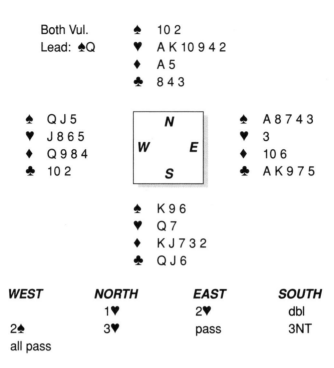

Both Vul.
Lead: ♠Q

	♠	10 2
	♥	A K 10 9 4 2
	♦	A 5
	♣	8 4 3

West:
♠ Q J 5
♥ J 8 6 5
♦ Q 9 8 4
♣ 10 2

East:
♠ A 8 7 4 3
♥ 3
♦ 10 6
♣ A K 9 7 5

South:
♠ K 9 6
♥ Q 7
♦ K J 7 3 2
♣ Q J 6

WEST	NORTH	EAST	SOUTH
	1♥	2♥	dbl
2♠	3♥	pass	3NT
all pass			

Most players would bid on the East hand here. However, the consequences of doing so are not only to divert North-South from their normal (and failing) 4♥ contract, but also to provide a road map for an alert declarer.

East's 2♥ is a variation of the Michaels Cuebid, in this case showing at least five-five in the black suits. Your double shows defensive values without a good heart fit. When North rebids his hearts to show a good suit you realize that 4♥ may flounder on the rocks of unfriendly distribution. You also hope to be able to use East's bidding to your advantage in 3NT. This is a well-judged decision, as 4♥ fails on the obvious club ruff.

The opening ♠Q lead is ducked to your ♠K. You don't have many top tricks and the defense's spades are already established, so you will need either hearts or diamonds to run. How should you play the red suits to maximize your chances? If you think back to the bidding, you will realize that you know that East has at least ten black cards. Your first move should be to cash the ♥Q — if East discards you will have no choice but to play him for ♦Qxx. When he follows to the first heart, your prospects are excellent. You start by cashing the ♦AK. If East discards on either of these tricks, you intend to rely on hearts breaking 3-2. When he follows to both diamonds, you know his original pattern was 5-1-2-5, so you can lead a heart and confidently finesse dummy's ten.

The play of this hand was simplified by East's two-suited overcall. All you had to do was count to three — the number of red-suit cards he held. Yes, it can be that easy to count the hand after an opponent shows a five-five distribution during the auction.

Before giving you a hand to declare, we want to introduce you to a suit combination:

Dummy
♥ A 9 3

Declarer
♥ K J 2

At first sight, you might think that you have a 50-50 chance of making three tricks from this suit. Cashing the ace before taking the finesse marginally improves your chances since West may hold a singleton queen, but essentially you need East to hold the queen.

Obviously, if you can persuade West to lead the suit, you will make three tricks irrespective of how the defenders' cards lie. However, the presence of the nine in dummy also means that your chances are greatly improved if East can be forced to open up the suit.

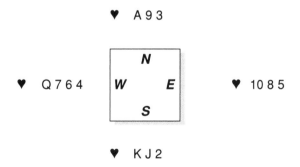

♥ A 9 3

♥ Q 7 6 4   ♥ 10 8 5

♥ K J 2

Even though a simple finesse for the queen would lose, dummy's nine enables you to make three tricks if RHO leads the suit and you play low from hand. Try it and see. Of course, if the queen and ten were switched, you would win West's ♥10 with the ace and still be able to finesse the jack on the next round. Remember this suit combination: it will help you make the next hand.

N-S Vul. ♠ K 4 3
Lead: ♣K ♥ A 9 6
          ♦ A 8 3 2
          ♣ 4 3 2

          ♠ A Q 6 5 2
          ♥ K J 5
          ♦ K 4
          ♣ A 7 5

WEST	NORTH	EAST	SOUTH
			1♠
2NT[1]	dbl[2]	pass	pass
3♣	3♠	pass	3NT
all pass			

1. Minors
2. Defensive values, but no good spade fit

North was reluctant to forego a vulnerable game for what might prove an indifferent penalty and now it's up to you to justify his decision. You duck the opening ♣K lead, but take the club continuation since you know from the bidding that East has, at most, a doubleton. Counting your tricks, you can see eight on top — three spades, two diamonds, two hearts and one club. It looks straightforward to develop your ninth trick in spades, but when you play a spade to dummy's king, West discards a diamond. Well, at least you're not in 4♠! The heart suit will now have to furnish your ninth trick, but can you see anything better than simply playing East for the queen?

West's bidding showed at least five cards in each minor. East followed to the second club, so West had only five of those, and when you play off the top diamonds, East again follows twice. Since West had no spades he was 0-3-5-5. East, therefore, began with a 5-4-2-2 shape. Armed with this knowledge, and remembering the suit combination we talked about earlier, can you see a way to make the hand as long as East holds either the ♥Q or the ♥10?

You need four more tricks. This is the position when you play a spade to your queen (each '?' represents a card that is either the ♥Q, the ♥10 or a small heart):

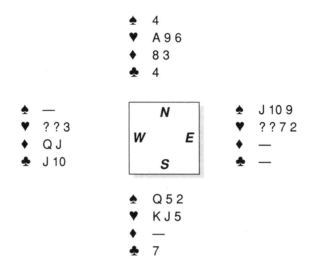

```
                    ♠   4
                    ♥   A 9 6
                    ♦   8 3
                    ♣   4

        ♠   —                      ♠   J 10 9
        ♥   ? ? 3      N           ♥   ? ? 7 2
        ♦   Q J    W       E       ♦   —
        ♣   J 10                   ♣   —
                       S
                    ♠   Q 5 2
                    ♥   K J 5
                    ♦   —
                    ♣   7
```

East is out of both minors and, when you now play the last spade winner, West must decide how many hearts to retain. If he keeps all three hearts and throws a minor-suit winner, you intend to exit with a club. After taking his three tricks, West will have to lead a heart around to your king-jack.

But West thwarts this plan by discarding a heart and keeping four winners in clubs and diamonds, so you exit with a spade. East wins and cashes his last spade winner but then has to lead a heart, which you duck in hand. If West produces the ♥Q, you are home. If he can play the ♥10, you win the ♥A and finesse the ♥J coming back. You will go down if West has both the queen and ten of hearts, but that's much better than just relying on East to hold the ♥Q.

It is not only two-suited bids that make declarer's counting job easier. An opponent's preempt may give you headaches in the auction, but if you buy the contract, the bidding is likely to assist you in the play. While you may not know quite so much initially about the distribution as you did after the two-suited bids in the last two hands, a preempt gives you numerous clues about both defenders' hands and will often enable you to avoid a losing line of play. This is particularly so if the preempt is a closely defined bid such as a weak two.

Here is a straightforward example:

```
Both Vul.          ♠  —
Lead: ♥2           ♥  9 8 6 5
                   ♦  A 9 8 2
                   ♣  A 10 6 4 3

♠  K Q J 8 4 3        N          ♠  10 9 7 6 5
♥  2                             ♥  A Q 7 4 3
♦  Q 6 5 4        W       E      ♦  10
♣  9 2               S          ♣  7 5

                   ♠  A 2
                   ♥  K J 10
                   ♦  K J 7 3
                   ♣  K Q J 8
```

WEST	NORTH	EAST	SOUTH
2♠	pass	4♠	dbl
pass	4NT	pass	5♣
all pass			

East takes the first trick with the ♥A and returns the suit. West ruffs your jack and exits with the ♠K. You ruff in dummy and draw trumps, West discarding a spade on the second round.

Taken in isolation, the normal way to play the diamond suit for no losers would be to cash the ace and lead towards your king-jack, intending to finesse. As you can see, that would not work here. A little counting will tell you what to do, though.

West's Weak Two opening bid showed a six-card spade suit. He has subsequently shown up with just one heart and a doubleton club, and hence his original shape was 6-1-4-2. If West has both the queen and the ten of diamonds, then you cannot prevent him from scoring a trick in the suit. But if East's singleton is either of those cards, you can score four diamond tricks by cashing the king first, then finessing through West — which works as the cards lie here. You are able to play the diamond suit here in an unorthodox fashion only because you knew the distribution of the defenders' cards in the suit.

A three-level preempt doesn't give you quite as much information as does a well-defined convention like a Weak Two, but nevertheless it can be very helpful to an alert declarer. Often, the information you gain will steer you away from a losing option.

```
Neither Vul.        ♠  Q 10 9 6
Lead: ♠5            ♥  A 4
                    ♦  Q 6 3
                    ♣  A K 8 4

                 ┌─────────┐
                 │    N    │
                 │ W     E │
                 │    S    │
                 └─────────┘

                    ♠  A K J 8 4
                    ♥  K 8 6 5
                    ♦  —
                    ♣  Q 10 6 2
```

WEST	NORTH	EAST	SOUTH
		3♥	3♠
pass	4NT[1]	pass	6♦[2]
pass	7♠	all pass	

1. Roman Key Card Blackwood
2. Two key cards and a diamond void

All that remains is for you to justify North's faith in your declarer play. Counting your winners you see that thirteen tricks are possible via a number of routes. One option is to ruff two hearts in dummy, but for that to work you need trumps 2-2 as West will have, at most, one heart (and probably none, since he didn't lead one). A more attractive alternative is to reverse the dummy — you will try to score three diamond ruffs in hand, four trump tricks in dummy, two top hearts and four clubs.

Since you need entries to the North hand to take three ruffs, you win trick one with dummy's ♠9 and immediately ruff a diamond with a high spade. When you lead a small trump to the ten both defenders follow. You ruff a second diamond, cross to the ♥A (West discarding a diamond), and ruff dummy's third diamond with your last trump, both defenders following.

So far so good. Now you just need clubs to break 3-2 and you're home — right? Before you cash the top clubs though, stop to count. These cards remain:

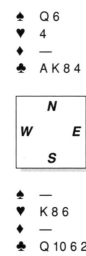

```
        ♠ Q 6
        ♥ 4
        ♦ —
        ♣ A K 8 4


              N
          W       E
              S


        ♠ —
        ♥ K 8 6
        ♦ —
        ♣ Q 10 6 2
```

East has followed to two spades and three diamonds. You also know East began with seven hearts since West showed out on the first round. That's twelve of his cards already accounted for, so he can have, at most, one club. Having reached this conclusion, you cash the ♣Q, West playing the ♣5 and East the ♣3. When you lead a second club, West follows with the ♣7, but you play the ♣8 from dummy, certain that it will win! This is the full hand:

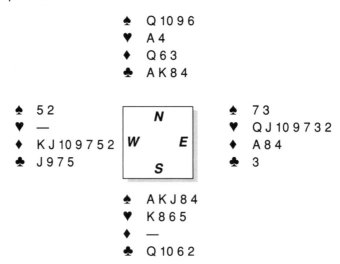

```
                   ♠ Q 10 9 6
                   ♥ A 4
                   ♦ Q 6 3
                   ♣ A K 8 4

    ♠ 5 2                              ♠ 7 3
    ♥ —              N                 ♥ Q J 10 9 7 3 2
    ♦ K J 10 9 7 5 2   W     E         ♦ A 8 4
    ♣ J 9 7 5              S           ♣ 3

                   ♠ A K J 8 4
                   ♥ K 8 6 5
                   ♦ —
                   ♣ Q 10 6 2
```

Note that had you drawn trumps and ruffed two hearts in dummy, you would not have discovered the unfavorable club break until it was too late to do anything about it.

Our next deal contains a number of points, some of which are quite advanced. First though, take a look at these common suit combinations:

Dummy

♦   A 6 4

Declarer

♦   Q J 5 3

Perhaps your first reaction is 'ah, a finesse' — so you lead the queen, intending to run it if West does not cover. Before you do that, ask yourself what you are hoping for.

If West has the king he will simply cover your queen, so you can never make more than three tricks, irrespective of how the opponents' cards are distributed. Your best chance is to find East with the king, which will enable you to score three tricks even when the suit breaks 4-2 (or worse).

The correct play is low to the ace and then back towards the QJ. If your queen wins, then you plan to re-enter dummy in another suit and lead towards the jack. By following this plan you will make three tricks whenever the suit breaks 3-3 or East holds the king. The key is to lead *towards* your honors.

Before going on, let's examine another simple suit combination:

Dummy

♦   A Q 6 4

Declarer

♦   J 8 3

A 3-3 break will again produce four tricks, but this time you cannot lead twice towards your minor honors. Now, it seems that if the missing cards split 4-2 you need to find a defender with Kx. Things are not always quite that simple, and applying the principles discussed above may still enable you to sidestep fate's intention. However, in our next example, correct handling of this suit followed by an endplay enables you to bring home a seemingly impossible contract by offering East a choice of unpalatable options.

Neither Vul.
Lead: ♣J

♠ K Q 8 2
♥ A 8
♦ A Q 6 4
♣ 8 7 3

♠ A 9 6 5 4 3
♥ Q 5
♦ J 8 3
♣ A K

WEST	NORTH	EAST	SOUTH
3♥	dbl	pass	5♠
pass	6♠	all pass	

You win Trick 1 in hand with a high club, perforce, and count your tricks — six spades, two clubs, one heart and one diamond comes to ten. You need to find two more tricks and those can only come from the red suits.

After drawing trumps with the ♠AK (West following twice and East discarding a club), you play a club to the king, then a spade back to dummy and ruff the third club. This effort is rewarded when West discards a heart. You can infer that West had seven hearts from his bid, and you now know he started with exactly two cards in each black suit, and therefore only two diamonds.

If your assumptions are correct, the remaining cards are as shown in the diagram.

(See diagram at the top of the next page.)

Can you see a way to make six of the last seven tricks no matter who has the king of diamonds?

Let's say you play a diamond to the ace and then a small diamond from dummy. If West has the ♦K, he will win and will have to to lead a heart away from the king. What if East has the ♦K?

Move around to the East seat momentarily — do you see his dilemma? If

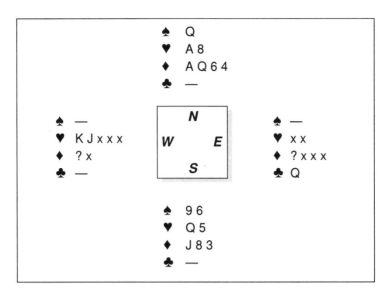

he wins the ♦K and returns a heart, you win dummy's ace, cash the ♦J, then cross back to dummy in trumps to discard your heart loser on ♦Q. If East instead refuses to take his ♦K, your jack will win. You then play ace and another heart, leaving West on lead with only hearts left, and the forced ruff and discard will allow you to dispose of your losing diamond. Either way, the defense is powerless to prevent you from making twelve tricks.

The full hand was:

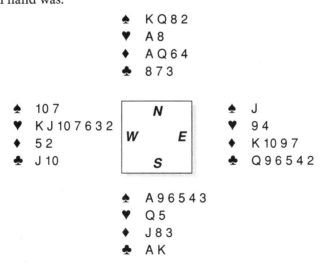

On our final deal in this chapter, counting the defenders' hands allows you to turn a 50-50 guess into a certainty:

Both Vul.
Lead: ♦J

♠ K Q 8 5 4
♥ A 7 4 3
♦ A 4
♣ K J

```
        N
   W        E
        S
```

♠ A 9 7 2
♥ Q 8 2
♦ 10 5
♣ A Q 10 4

WEST	NORTH	EAST	SOUTH
		3♦	dbl
pass	4♦	pass	4♠
pass	4NT	pass	5♥
pass	6♠	all pass	

You have only eleven tricks and there is only one real hope for a twelfth — lead towards the ♥Q and hope East has the king. Or is there? You win the ♦A and draw trumps in three rounds, East following once and then discarding two diamonds. You cash four clubs, throwing dummy's diamond. East follows to all four clubs while West pitches a heart on the fourth round. You ruff your losing diamond in dummy, both defenders following. You are at the critical point of the hand, but you have also discovered everything you need to know.

♠ 5
♥ A 7 4
♦ —
♣ —

```
        N
   W        E
        S
```

♠ 7
♥ Q 8 2
♦ —
♣ —

West's ♦J lead must be from a doubleton — he would lead small from ♦Jxx and he couldn't have ♦J10x as you had the ten — so East started with seven diamonds. He also followed to four rounds of clubs and one spade, leaving him room for just a singleton heart. The contract is now 100%. Do you see how?

Watch what happens when you lead a small heart from dummy and follow small from your hand too! Whichever defender wins the trick will be endplayed. If East wins, he has only diamonds left and the forced ruff and discard allows you to throw your second heart loser. If West overtakes his partner's card, he will have to return a heart away from the king and you will score the ♥Q as your twelfth trick. Here is the full hand:

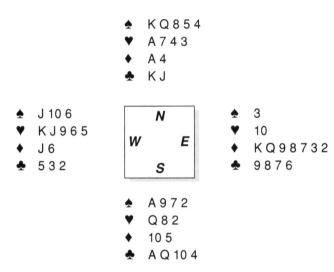

```
                    ♠  K Q 8 5 4
                    ♥  A 7 4 3
                    ♦  A 4
                    ♣  K J

     ♠  J 10 6          N          ♠  3
     ♥  K J 9 6 5                  ♥  10
     ♦  J 6        W       E       ♦  K Q 9 8 7 3 2
     ♣  5 3 2                      ♣  9 8 7 6
                        S

                    ♠  A 9 7 2
                    ♥  Q 8 2
                    ♦  10 5
                    ♣  A Q 10 4
```

As these deals illustrate, when a defender has made an informative bid such as a preempt or a two-suited overcall, you can usually get a count of the defenders' distribution early in the hand. Knowing the shape of the closed hands will often enable you to make a contract that goes down at other tables. Less successful declarers will have failed for one of two possible reasons. The first is because their opponents' bidding did not provide sufficient information to direct them to the winning line of play. That is understandable. The second possibility, which is that declarer did not make the effort to count, is not.

Sadly, all too often, it is the latter reason that is likely to be the true one. While counting cards at Blackjack may be frowned upon by those in authority, doing so at the bridge table is not only permitted but positively encouraged.

- Think about potential play problems *during* the bidding. Use the information provided by the opponents' bidding to envisage how the play is likely to go, and bid accordingly.

- If a defender has shown two suits in the bidding, concentrate on uncovering the distribution of his short suits.

- It is always best if the opponents lead suits in which you have tenace positions. Use your knowledge of the defenders' shapes to leave them on lead at the critical moment.

- Delay playing the crucial suit until you have gathered all available information.

- Avoid relying on cards to lie favorably unless that is your *only* chance. Counting the defenders' shapes frequently provides a better alternative.

CHAPTER 6

Clues from the Opening Lead

During the play of a bridge hand, declarer has the significant advantage of being able to see all of his assets. In order to equalize matters, good defenders pass information to one another by signalling with their spot cards. However, since declarer can see the same signals, a defender must weigh the value of keeping partner informed against the need to conceal his holdings from an inquisitive declarer. On most hands, competent partnerships signal honestly in the early play, and particularly on the opening lead.

In previous chapters we have examined various techniques you can use to count the defenders' hands. Information gleaned from the opening lead is another piece in that puzzle. Consider this everyday play problem:

```
Neither Vul.        ♠  A Q J 3
Lead: ♥3            ♥  8 6
                    ♦  A K 9 2
                    ♣  J 10 7
```

```
                    ♠  K 6
                    ♥  A 4 2
                    ♦  J 10 8 3
                    ♣  K Q 5 2
```

WEST	NORTH	EAST	SOUTH
			1♦
pass	1♠	pass	1NT
pass	3NT	all pass	

You have seven top tricks and the choice of either knocking out the ♣A or taking the diamond finesse to establish the extra two tricks you need. Which option do you choose?

The first question you should ask is, 'What lead style do the opponents play?' If they lead fourth-best from length, you can reasonably expect hearts to be 4-4 (although there is a chance that West has led a three-card suit). East plays the ♥K at trick one and, when that holds, he returns the ♥5. When you duck again, West wins the ♥10 and plays a third heart to your ace. Hearts appear to be 4-4, so it is safe to establish your extra tricks by knocking out the ♣A. All the defense can take is one club and three hearts.

Let's alter the early play so that West leads the ♥5 to his partner's queen. East returns ♥10 and West follows with the ♥3 when you duck again. East's ♥9 now forces your ace. This time it looks certain that hearts are 5-3. If West has the ♣A, then trying to establish your extra tricks in that suit will be fatal as he will win his ace and cash two more heart tricks. Your best chance is that West holds the ♦Q. After winning the ♥A, cash a top diamond (in case the queen is singleton), cross back to the ♠K, and take a diamond finesse. This line of play will work unless East has the ♦Q *and* West has the ♣A as an entry to his long hearts.

Finally, consider how you would play if West starts the ♥Q, which you allow to hold as East signals with the seven. West continues with the ♥3 to his partner's king and again you duck. East returns the ♥5 to your ace and West follows with the ♥9. Do you knock out the ♣A or take the diamond finesse? Again, it appears that hearts are 4-4. Why? Because if West had ♥QJ1093 he would continue with an honor at trick two. If they are 3-5 that would mean West started with ♥Q93, from which he would normally lead low. It is thus correct to knock out the ♣A since taking a diamond finesse risks establishing a fifth winner for the defense.

Sometimes it is not the card led, but the suit chosen which gives you a vital clue. Try your hand at this problem:

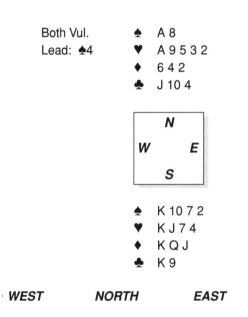

Both Vul.
Lead: ♠4

♠ A 8
♥ A 9 5 3 2
♦ 6 4 2
♣ J 10 4

♠ K 10 7 2
♥ K J 7 4
♦ K Q J
♣ K 9

WEST	NORTH	EAST	SOUTH
			1NT
pass	2♦[1]	pass	3♥[2]
pass	4♥	all pass	

1. Transfer
2. Maximum and good heart fit

You win East's ♠Q with the king. You have four possible losers — two minor-suit aces plus the ♥Q and the ♣Q. You plan to play trumps from the top, so you cash the king first in case either defender is void. Everyone follows to the ♥K, but on the second trump West's ♥10 forces the ace and East discards a diamond. You now have three certain losers.

You cross to the ♠A and play a diamond. West wins the ♦A, cashes the ♥Q, and exits with a second diamond. When you lead a spade to ruff in dummy, West follows with the jack, establishing your ♠10. You play a third round of diamonds, on which West discards a club, and lead out the ♠10. West discards another club and you ruff your winner in dummy so that you can lead the ♣J. You now know the whole hand except which defender has which club honor:

Is there anything to guide you?

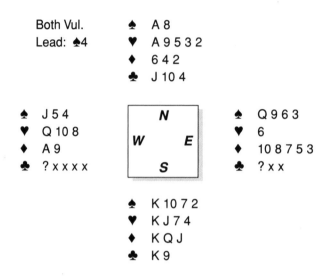

```
Both Vul.          ♠  A 8
Lead: ♠4           ♥  A 9 5 3 2
                   ♦  6 4 2
                   ♣  J 10 4

   ♠  J 5 4            N            ♠  Q 9 6 3
   ♥  Q 10 8                        ♥  6
   ♦  A 9         W       E         ♦  10 8 7 5 3
   ♣  ? x x x x       S             ♣  ? x x

                   ♠  K 10 7 2
                   ♥  K J 7 4
                   ♦  K Q J
                   ♣  K 9
```

What about the bidding? Would either defender have bid with the ♣A rather than the queen? No, so there's no help there. Is there anything in the play to guide you? What about West's opening ♠4 lead? Leads from holdings such as Jxx are notoriously poor choices, and are often an indicator of unpleasant alternatives. Here, a trump from ♥Q10x is out of the question, as is leading an unsupported ace with the strong hand on the right. However, leading from ♣Qxxxx would be far less dangerous than a spade from ♠Jxx. The most likely explanation for West's actual choice is that his clubs are headed by the ace rather than the queen. You therefore run the ♣J, and when that forces West's ace you are home.

Inferences of this kind will not always lead you to the winning conclusion. Indeed, the standard of the opposition has a bearing on the validity of any such deductions. However, when all else appears equal you must use whatever information you have, no matter how tenuous it may be. Inferences from the lead can sometimes suggest the shape of the defender's hand. With that clue, try this next problem:

Both Vul.   ♠ K J 8 2
Lead: ♣Q   ♥ K Q 10 4
            ♦ Q 3
            ♣ 10 8 4

           ♠ 9 6 5
           ♥ A 8 6
           ♦ A J 10 4
           ♣ A 7 5

WEST	NORTH	EAST	SOUTH
		pass	1♦
pass	1♥	pass	1NT
pass	2NT	pass	3NT
all pass			

East plays the ♣6 and you allow the queen to hold. You duck again when West continues with the ♣J, East completing a high-low with the ♣3. Trick three goes ♣9-♣10-♣K-♣A. You cross to the ♥K to lead the ♦Q, which loses to West's king. When the ♠3 comes back you have reached the first hurdle. Is this a normal king-jack guess, though?

You have lost three tricks, and the ♠A and the thirteenth club are still out-standing. Since the long club represents the setting trick, West would have cashed it if he had it, and East's initial high-low also suggests that he began with four clubs. If East has the ♠A as an entry, you are doomed no matter what you do. Therefore, you must assume West has that card. You could choose to play West for both the ace and the queen of spades. However, as you can reasonably expect to score four heart tricks, this is an inferior option, so you rise with the ♠K and it holds.

You now have eight tricks — one club, one spade, three diamonds and three hearts. The fate of the contract depends on making a fourth heart trick. You cross back to hand with the ♥A and cash your diamonds, on the last of which West pitches a spade. You must now decide whether the position is:

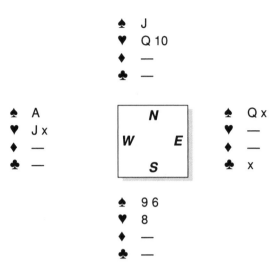

in which case you must take a heart finesse. Or:

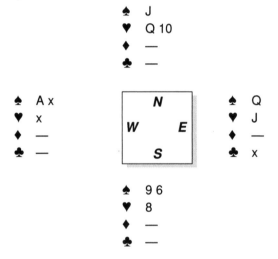

in which case playing for hearts to break evenly is the winning option.

Playing for hearts to have been 3-3 (or for the two outstanding cards to break 1-1) is the percentage play, but the odds are extremely close. Is there anything to guide you?

Let's construct the two possible West hands:

♠ A x x	♠ A x x x
♥ J x x x *or*	♥ x x x
♦ K x x	♦ K x x
♣ Q J 9	♣ Q J 9

West would not have bid on either hand, so there are no clues there. However, on this auction many players would prefer to lead an unbid four-card major rather than a three-card minor. Perhaps some would still lead a club with the second hand, but surely the odds favor West's holding the first hand. You lead a heart to the ten and when East discards you claim your contract.

The more you know about the defenders' hands, the easier your task; but it is important to realize that your opponents release information in two ways — under their own control and by default. In Chapter 10 we shall see how you might use the defenders' signals to your advantage, and how you can encourage them to signal accurately in key situations. However, all information is not of equal value. If a player fails to follow suit then there is only one explanation — he does not have any more cards in that suit. That is guaranteed. You must be more wary when drawing conclusions from information *volunteered* by a defender. In this, bridge is not unlike 'real life', as you often have to determine the reliability of information based on the source.

Often, you cannot get a complete count of the hand, but you can gather sufficient information to make an 'educated guess' — an informed decision that will be right most of the time. Such choices are often based on the 'Theory of Vacant Spaces'. The premise for this theory is that if West has, for example, eight unknown cards and East has only four, then West is twice as likely (8 to 4 or 2 to 1) to hold a specific missing card.

This is absolutely true. However, a little learning can be a dangerous thing. Consider the following hand from a team-of-four match:

```
Neither Vul.      ♠  A 6 3
Lead: ♠5          ♥  J 7 3
                  ♦  A J 8 5 4
                  ♣  K 10
```

```
            N
        W       E
            S
```

```
                  ♠  J 8 2
                  ♥  A 8 5
                  ♦  K 10 6 3
                  ♣  A 7 3
```

WEST	NORTH	EAST	SOUTH
	1♦	pass	3NT
all pass			

East wins the ♠Q and returns the ♠9. West overtakes with the ♠10 and you duck again. A third round of spades forces dummy's ace as East discards a heart. If you misguess the diamonds, your contract will fail. How do you tackle the diamonds? West has five spades to East's two, and thus East has eleven non-spades (or vacant spaces) to West's eight. It is therefore obviously the right percentage play to cash the ♦A and then finesse through East for the ♦Q on the second round... Or is it?

Before deciding, take the North seat at the second table in the same match. This time, the bidding is:

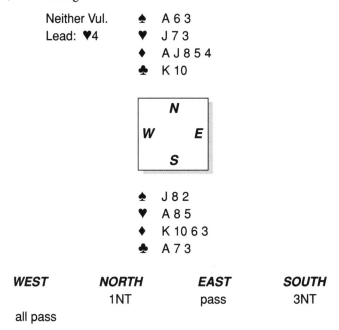

Neither Vul.
Lead: ♥4

```
        ♠  A 6 3
        ♥  J 7 3
        ♦  A J 8 5 4
        ♣  K 10


        ♠  J 8 2
        ♥  A 8 5
        ♦  K 10 6 3
        ♣  A 7 3
```

WEST	NORTH	EAST	SOUTH
	1NT	pass	3NT
all pass			

North-South at this table are playing a 12-14 1NT, so you become declarer from the North seat in the same 3NT contract.

East leads the ♥4 and you duck your ace until the third round, discovering in the process that West has only a doubleton heart. How do you tackle the diamonds? Since East has five hearts to West's two, West has eleven non-hearts (or vacant spaces) to East's eight. It is therefore obviously the right percentage play to cash the ♦K and then finesse through West for the ♦Q on the second round...

Ah! We seem to have been here before. One of these two declarers is destined to go down, yet both have apparently taken the correct line of play. How curious! This situation is often called the 'Monty Hall Trap' after the host of a well-known American TV game-show. For readers who may not have seen Monty Hall's show, the idea was for a contestant to guess which of three doors concealed the grand prize. The other two hid only booby prizes. To add spice to the show, Monty Hall tempted the contestants by offering to buy their choice from them before they knew if they had a winner. The mathematical aspects of the problem as they relate to bridge were first addressed by Phil Martin of New York in a 1990 *Bridge Today* article. A precis of the opening part of Martin's article illustrates the problem:

'Behind one of these doors,' shouts Monty Hall, 'is the grand prize worth $100,000! It's all yours — if you pick the right door.'

'I'll take Door Number One,' you say.

'Before we look,' says Monty. 'I'll offer you $20,000 for whatever is behind Door Number One.'

'Of course not,' you say. 'Even assuming the booby prizes are worth nothing, the expected value of my choice is $33,333. Why should I take $20,000?'

'All right,' says Monty. 'But before we see what you've won, let's take a look behind Door Number Two.'

Predictably, Door Two opens to reveal one of the two booby prizes.

'I'll give you one last chance,' says Monty Hall. 'You can have $40,000 for what's behind Door Number One.'

Should you take it? It would seem that you now have a 50:50 shot at the $100,000, and so you should refuse the $40,000. That would be true if Monty Hall had chosen a door at random. But he didn't. Monty knows which door conceals the grand prize, and (showman that he is) he intentionally showed you a booby prize to heighten the suspense.

Two of the doors were known to conceal a booby prize. When you chose door one, you knew that at least one of the other doors hid a booby prize. The only difference is that you now know Door Two *did*. Monty could just as easily have shown you a booby prize behind Door Three. Whether Door One or Door Three hides the $100,000, there was no chance it would be behind the door Monty opened. In reality, you have learned nothing and you still have the same one-in-three chance you started with. The winning strategy is therefore to take the $40,000, since the value of your choice is still the same $33,333 it was earlier. And by the way, the value of the other unopened door is indeed the missing $66,666. Sometimes Monty would offer you the chance to switch your choice at this point, and the odds are 2 to 1 in favor of doing so.

While this may be crystal clear to mathematicians, perhaps bridge players might relate more easily to the Restricted Choice implications. If Door Three hides the grand prize, then in order to show you a booby prize Monty *has* to open Door Two, and vice versa. However, if the grand prize is behind Door One he might equally have opened Door Two or Door Three. It therefore follows, in the actual situation, that the grand prize is twice as likely to be behind Door Three as behind Door One. You therefore still have only a 33.333% chance that Door One is the right one to choose.

This scenario exemplifies a classic probability trap — treating biased information as random. In the game show context, Monty Hall showed the contents of Door Two *because* it contained a booby prize. *The information itself had a direct bearing on whether you received it*, and that must be taken into account when assessing its value.

In bridge, many players overuse strategies designed to mislead. Such tactics fare better against unknown opponents because they are more likely to treat the information at face value. Using them against regular opponents is more likely to backfire, as they will make adjustments for bias in the data. The inevitable fate of Victor Mollo's Papa the Greek when he plays against the Hideous Hog is a classic example of this. The Hog knows that Papa can be relied on to try to deceive him, and acts accordingly.

Returning to the hand above, we can see that each declarer is faced with a similar problem, but that the information available apparently suggests opposite lines of play. Clearly, if both declarers base their play on 'vacant spaces theory' using only the information provided by the opening lead, one will go down. The reason for this is that the distribution of the suit that was led is *biased information*. It is not random at all. What has really happened? Yes, the defender on lead led his longest suit. That is a common enough occurrence, so why should you be surprised because he has more cards in that suit than his partner?

Go back to the first layout (when South became declarer). What if West had still led a spade but the suit had broken 4-3? West would still have nine unknown cards to East's ten, but in fact the true odds would favor playing West for the ♦Q. Why? Because West has presumably led his longest suit — spades — in which he has only four. West, therefore, does not have five hearts or five clubs and may well have no more than three of either suit. The only time he will have a singleton diamond is when he is precisely 4-4-1-4, and then he might equally have chosen to lead from a four-card heart or club suit.

All that may make things seem much more complicated than they really are. In an attempt to correct this impression, we ask you to try the hand at the top of the next page.

West's lead of the ♣3 has given nothing away. You have six top tricks and you can make three more tricks by finding the ♦Q. If you do lose a diamond, then your ninth trick will have to come from one of the majors.

East-West are playing third and fifth leads, so you can place West with five clubs and East with two. Using a simple vacant spaces argument, West has eight places for the ♦Q and East has eleven. Consequently it might seem right to play East for the missing queen. However, West had to lead *something*! Presumably, his holdings and the auction influenced the card he chose. You must therefore consider what choices West had before applying the vacant places argument.

Neither Vul.   ♠ 6 5 4
Lead: ♣3   ♥ Q 2
                ♦ K J 9 8 3
                ♣ A 7 2

```
        N
    W       E
        S
```

         ♠ K 8
         ♥ A 6 4 3
         ♦ A 10 5 4
         ♣ K Q 4

WEST	NORTH	EAST	SOUTH
			1NT
pass	3NT	all pass	

After this auction it would certainly be normal to lead a major, rather than a poor five-card club suit. To gauge the significance of this requires some knowledge of the opponents. For example, if West is the type of player who always leads from his longest suit against notrump, it is fairly close whether you should play for the ♦Q to be doubleton or for it to be with East. On the other hand, many experts would lead from a four-card major (or ♠QJx, ♠J10x or ♥J10x) before touching a jack-high club suit. Against them, you can assume West has at most six major-suit cards, giving East at least nine. This would leave West with *at least* two places for the ♦Q, and East with *at most* two. In such circumstances, it would be clear to play West for the ♦Q.

Most of the time, though, you will know little of West's proclivities. Our advice, then, is to play with the basic odds without reading too much into the tainted information. Attempting to work out why your partner has taken a particular action is hard enough, and you play with him every week. Trying to fathom why an unknown opponent has done something is more likely to give you a migraine than to solve the problem on the hand.

Thus, we can conclude that information you pry out of a defender (by making him follow suit) is reliable. Information he offers voluntarily may not be, and in any case is open to interpretation. When faced with such problems, you have to observe what happened and try to determine why the opponent has taken a particular action. Try to consider the opponent's alternatives and to gauge the most likely reason for the actions he took. Often the options will be sufficiently numerous that you can draw no definite conclusion. In such cases, you should rely heavily on the basic odds rather than on a tenuous inference from an opponent's action which may have been taken for one of any number of reasons.

LESSONS FROM THIS CHAPTER

- The opening lead and play to the early tricks will often tell you how the suit that has been led is breaking. From this, you will be able to tell how many winners the defenders have in the suit.

- When a defender leads from a dangerous holding (such as Jxx, Qxx or Axxx), ask yourself why. The reason will often be because other suits contained equally dangerous holdings.

- Beware of the 'Monty Hall Trap'. Defenders select their lead based on the auction and their hand. Do not apply vacant spaces theory based purely on a defender having length in the suit he chose to lead (or to bid).

- Information a defender offers voluntarily is open to interpretation. Always consider why the opponent has taken that particular action.

CHAPTER 7

Locating a Queen

It is surprising how often the success of a contract depends on locating a queen. There are two common positions. The first involves this type of holding, where you must decide whether to try to drop a doubleton queen offside or to take a finesse.

Dummy
♣ J 10 x x

Declarer
♣ A K x x x

The other type of hand is one on which you have a two-way finesse:

Dummy

♣ A J x (x)

Declarer

♣ K 10 x (x) (x)

What is your batting average in these situations? A little over 50%? Having failed in a contract because you did not find a queen, perhaps you can recall shrugging your shoulders and making a comment such as 'It was a complete guess.' But was that really the case? You might reflect on how expert opponents seem to have an uncanny ability to find these vital queens against you.

There are several techniques you can employ to improve your success rate on these hands. They all involve counting of one sort or another. Sometimes, a contract that appears to depend on a guess becomes a certainty.

E-W Vul.
Lead: ♣Q

	♠	K J 7 3
	♥	A K J 9 2
	♦	A 7 2
	♣	7

♠ Q 9 8 5 2		♠ 6
♥ 6		♥ Q 7 5 4 3
♦ 9		♦ J 10 8 4 3
♣ Q J 9 8 5 2		♣ 10 6

	♠	A 10 4
	♥	10 8
	♦	K Q 6 5
	♣	A K 4 3

WEST	NORTH	EAST	SOUTH
			1NT
pass	2♦	pass	2♥
pass	2♠	pass	2NT
pass	3♦	pass	3NT
pass	6NT	all pass	

Your 1NT opening shows 15-17 points. North transfers to hearts, bids a natural and game-forcing 2♣, and shows his diamond fragment at his third turn. When you deny a fit for any of his suits, he raises to the notrump slam.

You win West's ♣Q with the ♣K and run the ♥10 to East's queen. East returns a club, completing a high-low, and you win the ace. You can count eleven tricks — four hearts, three diamonds, two clubs and two spades. If diamonds are 3-3 you will be able to claim; otherwise, you must find the ♠Q. You play off the top diamonds and West throws a spade on the second round. Your immediate thought may be that he wouldn't discard from the queen. When West throws another spade on the third diamond winner, you may now be convinced that East has the ♠Q. So, you lead a spade to the king and finesse the ten on the way back. How were you to know that West had eleven black cards and didn't bid over 1NT?

Unlucky? Not at all, because you broke the golden rule — delay the decision until the last possible moment. Having taken your diamond winners, there was no reason not to cash dummy's hearts too. When you played the second heart, West would discard a club and all would be clear. At that point you could count East's hand — five hearts, five diamonds, at least two clubs, and thus at most one spade. It would then be routine to cash the ♠A (in case East's singleton was the queen) and to finesse dummy's ♠J knowing it will win.

Now consider this suit combination:

Dummy

♣ K J 6 2

Declarer

♣ A 9 7 4

To make four tricks, you seem to need a 3-2 break with West holding the queen. If the suit breaks 4-1, even a singleton queen with East does not help as you cannot pick up West's ♣10863. However, a singleton honor in the East hand is good enough, provided you start by cashing the right honor.

While getting a complete count of the defenders' hands is not uncommon, you may have to make your decision with only a partial count. Let's put this suit into a full hand:

While getting a complete count of the defenders' hands is not uncommon, often you will have to make your decision with only a partial count, as here:

Both Vul.
Lead: ♥J

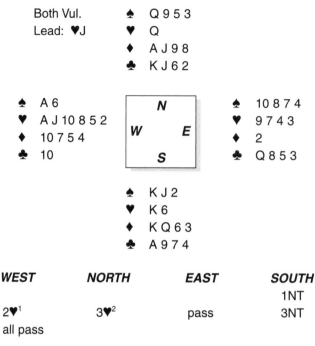

```
              ♠  Q 9 5 3
              ♥  Q
              ♦  A J 9 8
              ♣  K J 6 2

♠  A 6                        ♠  10 8 7 4
♥  A J 10 8 5 2    N          ♥  9 7 4 3
♦  10 7 5 4    W     E        ♦  2
♣  10              S          ♣  Q 8 5 3

              ♠  K J 2
              ♥  K 6
              ♦  K Q 6 3
              ♣  A 9 7 4
```

WEST	NORTH	EAST	SOUTH
			1NT
2♥[1]	3♥[2]	pass	3NT
all pass			

1. Natural
2. Stayman, denying a heart stopper

Dummy's ♥Q wins Trick 1, and East plays the ♥7, suggesting an even number. You have seven top tricks, but with hearts now wide open you cannot afford to knock out the ♠A. The two extra tricks you require will have to come from the club suit. It looks obvious to cash the ♣A, intending to finesse against West on the second round, particularly since East cannot have many high cards. After all, he passed despite holding four-card heart support. However, there is no rush to play clubs. Remembering our advice to delay playing key suits, you cash the ♦AK and East surprises you by discarding a heart. You now know that West started with ten red cards. In view of East's silence, West must also have the ♠A. That leaves just two unknown cards in West's hand.

There are three indicators that West's original shape was 2-6-4-1 rather than 1-6-4-2. First, since there are six spades and only five clubs outstanding, West is slightly more likely to have two spades and one club. Also, perhaps East would have been more inclined to raise hearts with a 5-4-1-3 distribution than with 4-4-1-4 shape. (This will depend to some extent on East's style, since sacrifices against 3NT when the opponents have balanced hands are seldom successful, particularly at equal vulnerability.)

Having reached the conclusion that West is likely to hold a singleton club, you lead a low club from hand and West follows with the ten. He is five times more likely to hold ♠Ax and the ♣10 than precisely the ♠A and ♣Q10, so you rise with the ♣K and lead the ♣J. East follows low and when you run the jack, West discards. A club to the nine yields your ninth trick.

Once you know how a suit is breaking, the odds favor playing the defender with more cards in the suit for the missing queen. However, it is important not to play mechanically, allowing yourself to be blind to the implications of the information you have. With that hint, try this problem:

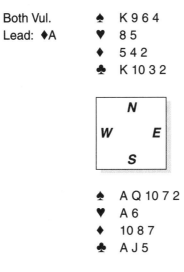

Both Vul.	♠	K 9 6 4
Lead: ♦A	♥	8 5
	♦	5 4 2
	♣	K 10 3 2

♠ A Q 10 7 2
♥ A 6
♦ 10 8 7
♣ A J 5

WEST	NORTH	EAST	SOUTH
1♦	pass	1♥	1♠
2♥	2♠	pass	4♠
all pass			

West fires away with the ♦AKQ, East pitching a heart on the third round. West shifts to the ♥2; you take East's queen with the ace and draw trumps in two rounds. With the information that West's heart raise promised four-card support, you can count the defenders' hands. West had with five diamonds and two spades, so he started with a 2-4-5-2 shape. How do you play the clubs?

The odds are 4-to-2 that East has the ♣Q. A count of West's points (♦AKQJ, ♠J, ♥J) confirms that he has his opening bid without the ♣Q. That was easy! You lead a club to the king and finesse the jack on the way back and...

Wait! If East has ♣Qxxx, can you make the hand? The answer is no, since you will make only three club tricks and you will still have a heart to lose. As you need four club tricks, the only hope is that West has a doubleton queen. Cash the ♣AK, and if West's queen comes down you will be able to throw your heart loser on dummy's ♣10. This is the complete deal:

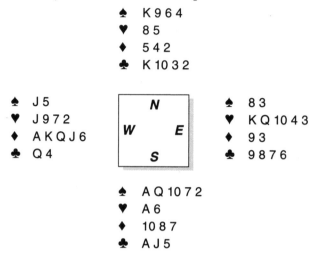

```
              ♠  K 9 6 4
              ♥  8 5
              ♦  5 4 2
              ♣  K 10 3 2

♠  J 5                          ♠  8 3
♥  J 9 7 2         N            ♥  K Q 10 4 3
♦  A K Q J 6    W     E         ♦  9 3
♣  Q 4                          ♣  9 8 7 6
                  S
              ♠  A Q 10 7 2
              ♥  A 6
              ♦  10 8 7
              ♣  A J 5
```

When you have a genuine two-way finesse, counting the defenders' distribution will not always pinpoint the missing queen. Sometimes you must work out the distribution and count the high card points to solve the conundrum. To close this chapter, try finding the ♥Q here:

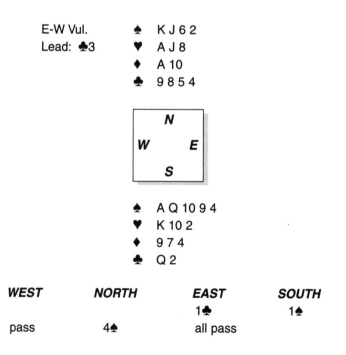

```
E-W Vul.      ♠  K J 6 2
Lead: ♣3      ♥  A J 8
              ♦  A 10
              ♣  9 8 5 4

                  N
              W       E
                  S

              ♠  A Q 10 9 4
              ♥  K 10 2
              ♦  9 7 4
              ♣  Q 2
```

WEST	NORTH	EAST	SOUTH
		1♣	1♠
pass	4♠	all pass	

East takes the ♣AK and switches to a trump. You have eight top tricks, and a diamond ruff will bring the total to nine, so you must find the ♥Q to make your contract. East's opening bid suggests that he is more likely to hold the key card but, of course, it is too early to commit yourself on that basis alone. There is still plenty of information to be gathered.

You win the trump in hand, play a diamond to the ace (East playing the jack), ruff a club high (West follows with the jack), and exit with a diamond to East's queen. East returns a second trump (to which West follows) and when you ruff your diamond loser, East contributes the king. You ruff dummy's last club and West discards a diamond.

You are down to one trump and three hearts in each hand. What do you know about the East hand? Clearly, he started with either 2-4-3-4 or 2-3-4-4 distribution. What about high cards? So far you have seen the ♣AK and the ♦KQJ — that's thirteen points. So, who has the ♥Q?

Curiously, this time the answer lies on the opponents' convention card. If they play a 15-17 1NT opening, you should play West for the ♥Q. If East has the ♥Q, then he started with a balanced fifteen-point hand and would presumably have opened 1NT. However, if the opponents are playing a 12-14 1NT you should play East for the missing queen: he opened 1♣ because he was too strong for 1NT.

If the opponents are playing a 15-17 1NT, the full hand would look something like this:

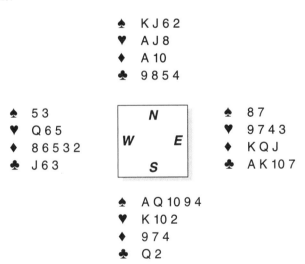

```
              ♠  K J 6 2
              ♥  A J 8
              ♦  A 10
              ♣  9 8 5 4

♠  5 3               N            ♠  8 7
♥  Q 6 5                          ♥  9 7 4 3
♦  8 6 5 3 2    W        E        ♦  K Q J
♣  J 6 3                          ♣  A K 10 7
                     S

              ♠  A Q 10 9 4
              ♥  K 10 2
              ♦  9 7 4
              ♣  Q 2
```

The primary lesson from these hands is to avoid committing yourself too early. By counting the defenders' distribution and high card points, it is possible to sniff out the majority of enemy queens.

LESSONS FROM THIS CHAPTER

- Delay making the crucial decision until the latest possible moment.

- Count the defenders' shapes and assume the hand with more cards in a suit will have the queen.

- Before playing a particular defender for the queen, make sure that doing so will solve your problem.

- **Remember the bidding.** Having mentally placed a key queen in a defender's hand, check that his previous actions are consistent with your conclusions.

CHAPTER 8

Looking for a Jack

It is easy to take your eye off the ball when your contract seems to have plenty of tricks. For example, how often have you mentally counted four tricks from the following suit combination?

Dummy
♣ A 10 4 3

Declarer
♣ K Q 9 5

About a quarter of the time, a defender will hold ♣Jxxx. That is too often to ignore and, when your contract goes down, shrug your shoulders and complain of 'bad breaks.' Even a partial count of the defenders' hands significantly improves your chance of taking four tricks. Clearly, the defender with fewer cards in the other suits is less likely to hold a singleton in this suit. This next example becomes fairly straightforward if you remember that:

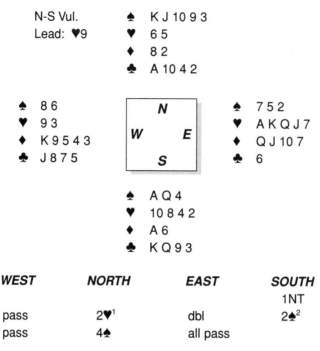

N-S Vul.
Lead: ♥9

North
♠ K J 10 9 3
♥ 6 5
♦ 8 2
♣ A 10 4 2

West
♠ 8 6
♥ 9 3
♦ K 9 5 4 3
♣ J 8 7 5

East
♠ 7 5 2
♥ A K Q J 7
♦ Q J 10 7
♣ 6

South
♠ A Q 4
♥ 10 8 4 2
♦ A 6
♣ K Q 9 3

WEST	NORTH	EAST	SOUTH
			1NT
pass	2♥[1]	dbl	2♠[2]
pass	4♠	all pass	

1. Transfer
2. At least three spades

West dutifully leads the ♥9. East takes the ♥J and ♥Q then shifts to the ♦Q. You have only nine top tricks so you are going to need four club tricks. You duck the first diamond and win the continuation, draw three rounds of trumps and ruff a heart (West discarding a diamond on the third round of both majors).

It is time to 'guess' the clubs. What do you know about the defenders' hands? East started with five hearts, three spades and at least two diamonds — ten non-clubs. He cannot possibly have four clubs, so you cash the two high clubs in hand and when East discards on the second round, you can take the proven finesse against West's ♣J.

It is even easier to be sloppy with a nine-card fit missing the jack. It would be unfortunate to go down on the next hand, but the sound practice of playing other suits before making the key decision should allow you to sidestep Lady Luck's outstretched foot.

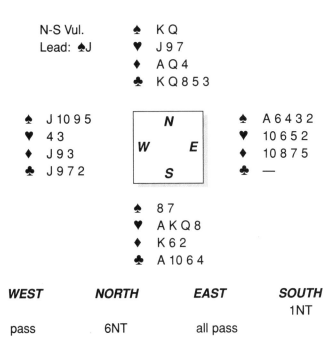

N-S Vul.
Lead: ♠J

♠ K Q
♥ J 9 7
♦ A Q 4
♣ K Q 8 5 3

♠ J 10 9 5
♥ 4 3
♦ J 9 3
♣ J 9 7 2

N
W   E
S

♠ A 6 4 3 2
♥ 10 6 5 2
♦ 10 8 7 5
♣ —

♠ 8 7
♥ A K Q 8
♦ K 6 2
♣ A 10 6 4

WEST	NORTH	EAST	SOUTH
			1NT
pass	6NT	all pass	

East takes the ♠A and returns the ♠3 to dummy's king. You seem to have tricks to burn — one spade, four hearts, three diamonds and five clubs comes to thirteen. The only thing that can possibly spike your guns is a 4-0 club break. Of course, you can pick up ♣J9xx in either defender's hand provided you cash the right honor first. You simply have to decide is which defender is more likely to be void. As it cannot cost to do a little investigating before touching clubs, you cash the ♦AQ and then play four rounds of hearts, throwing a club from dummy (you don't need a fifth club trick). West follows to two rounds of hearts and then discards the ♦J followed by a reluctant ♠10.

What do you know about the closed hands? It is reasonable to assume that East's ♠3 return was either an original fourth highest or from ♠A32. However, if East started with only three spades then West had six, which would have made two spade discards obvious and painless. Consequently, it seems that East has at least four spades. As he followed to two rounds of diamonds and four rounds of hearts, he cannot also have four clubs. Only West can have ♣J9xx. You cash the ♣A and are rewarded for your thoughtful play when East discards a spade. It is now a simple matter to lead the ♣10, covered by the jack and queen, then to re-enter your hand with the carefully preserved ♦K to repeat the club finesse.

On these deals you had a two-way finesse, but sometimes the choice is between finessing or playing for the jack to drop. Usually the suit looks something like this:

Dummy

♣ A Q 10 5

Declarer

♣ K 6 3

Having cashed the ♣AK, you lead towards the ♣Q10 and West plays the last small club. Did West start with ♣Jxxx or ♣xxx? The probabilities are extremely close. Unless the bidding or the play to this point suggests that West will be long in the suit, you should play for the drop. However, a count of the hand will often point you in the right direction.

Missing only five cards to the jack, the odds are not even close and it will be rare that you do anything except play for the drop. Occasionally, though, the bidding and early play may suggest you should ignore the normal percentages. On the next deal, one defender shows a two-suited hand during the bidding, and so he is known to be short in the key suit.

N-S Vul.	♠ Q 10 5		
Lead: ♣Q	♥ K Q 3		
	♦ 8 7 6 2		
	♣ 9 8 7		

West		East
♠ J 7 4 3		♠ 6
♥ 9 8 6 2	N	♥ 7 5
♦ 9 3	W E	♦ K Q J 10 4
♣ Q J 4	S	♣ A K 10 6 5

♠ A K 9 8 2
♥ A J 10 4
♦ A 5
♣ 3 2

WEST	NORTH	EAST	SOUTH
			1♠
pass	2♠	2NT[1]	dbl
3♣	pass	pass	4♠
all pass			

1. Minors

East overtakes the ♣Q and switches to the ♦K. The defenders have three obvious tricks, so you cannot afford a trump loser. The bidding makes it clear that if spades are 4-1 it is East who will be short, but should you play for the suit to break 3-2 or finesse against the jack? You win the ♦A and play the ♠A, both defenders producing small trumps. You lead a spade towards dummy and now you must decide...

East began with at most three major-suit cards. If two of those were spades, might he not have switched to his singleton heart at trick two, hoping to find his partner with a major-suit ace? This seems like such an obvious defense that you can probably rule out East having a 2-1-5-5 shape. Could East have started with ♠Jxx and no hearts? Perhaps, but would he then have overtaken the ♣Q? It seems more likely that he would have made a suit-preference signal at trick one in an attempt to get his partner to give him a ruff. Thus East's original distribution is unlikely to have been 3-0-5-5. As all the evidence points to a 4-1 spade break, you confidently put in the ♠10. When East discards, you draw trumps and claim your contract.

Sometimes you will have a choice of jacks to find. In such cases, it is best to delay the decision in the suit with the two-way guess. If it's not too early in the day, cover the defenders' hands and take declarer's seat for the next deal:

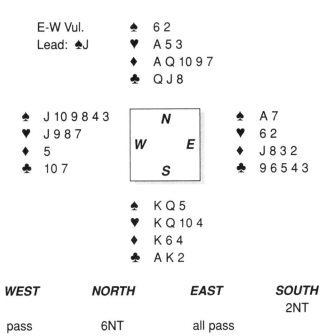

E-W Vul.
Lead: ♠J

North:
♠ 6 2
♥ A 5 3
♦ A Q 10 9 7
♣ Q J 8

West:
♠ J 10 9 8 4 3
♥ J 9 8 7
♦ 5
♣ 10 7

East:
♠ A 7
♥ 6 2
♦ J 8 3 2
♣ 9 6 5 4 3

South:
♠ K Q 5
♥ K Q 10 4
♦ K 6 4
♣ A K 2

WEST	NORTH	EAST	SOUTH
			2NT
pass	6NT	all pass	

East takes his ♠A and returns the ♠7 to your king. Counting your tricks, you can see two spades, three clubs, three hearts and three diamonds — eleven.

You have chances for a twelfth trick in both red suits, but which should you tackle first?

On general principles you should delay the decision in diamonds, where you have a two-way guess. You start by cashing the top hearts but East discards on the third round, so no joy there. Now you need a fourth diamond trick to bring home your slam. It cannot cost to cash your other spade winner, and when East throws another club, ten of West's cards are known — six spades and four hearts. Your contract is now 100% guaranteed. Do you see why?

To fill in the last part of the jigsaw, you cash the ♣AK (remembering to retain a late entry to dummy). If West discards on either club, then diamonds will break 3-2. When he follows to both clubs he cannot have more than one diamond, so you cross to the ♦A and confidently run the ♦10. You now cash the ♦K, cross back to dummy in clubs, and the ♦Q is your twelfth trick.

Sometimes your contract seems to depend on finding a jack well-placed. Appearances can be deceptive though...

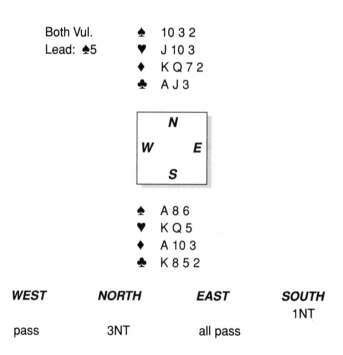

	Both Vul.	♠	10 3 2
	Lead: ♠5	♥	J 10 3
		♦	K Q 7 2
		♣	A J 3

♠	A 8 6
♥	K Q 5
♦	A 10 3
♣	K 8 5 2

WEST	NORTH	EAST	SOUTH
			1NT
pass	3NT	all pass	

You withhold your ♠A until the third round of spades, East playing the ♠Q and ♠7 before throwing a heart. Counting your tricks, you get to six — one spade, two clubs and three diamonds. It is conceivable that you can make your contract via four tricks in each minor, but that would require an extremely favorable position in both suits. A better shot is that East holds the ♥A so that you can safely establish two hearts to bring your total to eight tricks.

You lead the ♥K which holds, confirming that East has the ace. Now you play a club to the jack, since if it wins you can establish your ninth trick in hearts. However, East wins the ♣Q, cashes the ♥A, and exits with a heart (to which West follows). When you cash the ♣K, West discards a spade, so his original shape was 5-3-4-1. Given that West has four diamonds and East two, how should you play to optimize your chances?

Having come this far, many players would cash the ♦AK hoping to find East with ♦Jx, intending to use the ♣A as a dummy entry to overcome the diamond blockage. Alas, ♦Jx represents only one third (five of fifteen) of the possible doubletons East might hold. Can you improve on this 1-in-3 chance to make your game?

Try the effect of leading the ♦10, intending to run it if West follows with a small card. This plan relies on East having the doubleton nine or eight — a total of seven of the fifteen possible doubletons. You are still not a favorite to make four diamond tricks, but that's as good as it gets, and you are rewarded for playing with the odds when the full hand is:

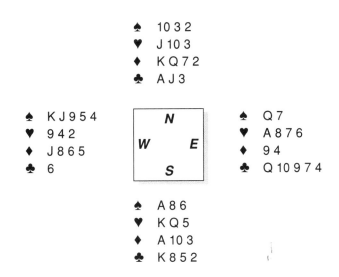

```
              ♠  10 3 2
              ♥  J 10 3
              ♦  K Q 7 2
              ♣  A J 3

   ♠  K J 9 5 4       N        ♠  Q 7
   ♥  9 4 2                     ♥  A 8 7 6
   ♦  J 8 6 5     W       E     ♦  9 4
   ♣  6                         ♣  Q 10 9 7 4
                       S
              ♠  A 8 6
              ♥  K Q 5
              ♦  A 10 3
              ♣  K 8 5 2
```

Discovering enough information to make consistently winning decisions in these situations requires some effort, but the ensuing rewards make the task well worthwhile.

LESSONS FROM THIS CHAPTER

- Check to see if it is possible to pick up Jxxx in *either* defender's hand.

- Be aware of how many entries are needed to pick up J9xx or J10xx.

- Counting a defender's cards in the other suits will often eliminate the possibility of him having Jxxx in the key suit. You can then guard against the other defender having that holding.

- Missing only four cards to the jack, try to eliminate the possibility of one defender being void in the suit.

- Before committing yourself, consider how a defender would have played if he had each of the possible hands.

- When you have a choice of jacks to find, delay the decision in the suit in which you have a two-way guess.

CHAPTER 9

Guessing King-Jack Combinations

ontinuing our discussion of situations in which success as declarer depends on locating key honor cards, we turn to one with which everyone is familiar, since it comes up so often: you need a trick from a suit in which you are missing both the ace and the queen. Once again, you've probably noticed that experts seem to get these decisions right more often than you do. Although these positions are often regarded as guesses, there is usually some clue to guide you. Indeed, in Chapter 6 we saw two examples that were resolved by counting. Here are the two basic king-jack combinations:

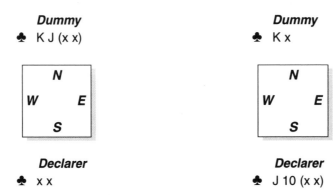

If one defender has both the ace and the queen, it won't matter what you do. It is when the missing honors are divided that your decision is crucial. It may be obvious to declarer that the contract depends on a correct 'guess' in this suit. However, the defenders may not know this yet, so the timing of when the suit is played may be critical. Psychological factors often figure in this decision.

In a suit contract, there are two ways to tackle these problems. One is to delay broaching the suit until the latest possible moment, expecting that by then you will have enough information to guess right. The disadvantage of this strategy is that competent defenders will also have worked out what is happening and West will always play low in tempo. The alternative is to lead the suit at the first opportunity hoping that West will give the position away if he has the ace. Early in a suit contract, defenders are under pressure not to let declarer play a suit such as the one below for one trick and no losers:

Most declarers will try to slip a trick through here before the defenders realize the situation; as a result, if the suit is played early on, West will often play the ace when he has it. Consequently, if he follows low smoothly, it is odds-on that the ace is over dummy.

Now consider West's play on this next suit combination:

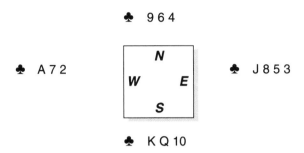

♣ 9 6 4

♣ A 7 2   ♣ J 8 5 3

♣ K Q 10

Let's say declarer wins trick one in dummy and immediately leads a low diamond to his king. If West wins his ace, then declarer is virtually forced into taking the winning finesse for the jack later. An expert West might smoothly duck his ace, and as a result declarer is very likely to misguess on the second round of the suit.

Now move back to declarer's seat. Can you now see the advantages of leading the following king-jack suit early, particularly if West is known to be an expert defender:

Dummy

♣   x x x

Declarer

♣   K J

If you lead towards the king-jack in the closed hand early in the play, it may appear to be a guess as to which honor to play. However, the king has a better chance of success. Why? Because, even if you have guessed wrong, a good West will sometimes duck with ♣Axx, hoping to leave you with a second-round guess when you have ♣KQ10.

Enough psychology! As this is a counting book, let's assume you prefer the technical approach of delaying the 'guess'.

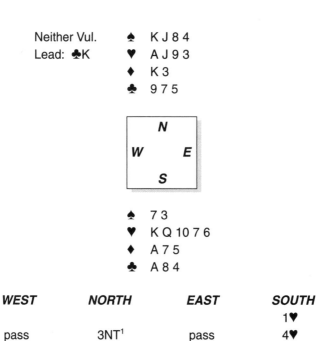

Neither Vul.
Lead: ♣K

♠ K J 8 4
♥ A J 9 3
♦ K 3
♣ 9 7 5

N
W   E
S

♠ 7 3
♥ K Q 10 7 6
♦ A 7 5
♣ A 8 4

WEST	NORTH	EAST	SOUTH
			1♥
pass	3NT[1]	pass	4♥
all pass			

1. Balanced raise to 4♥

You win the club lead and draw trumps in three rounds, East following while West pitches a club and a diamond. You seem destined to lose two clubs and the ♠A, so your contract depends on making a spade trick. You play off your top diamonds and ruff the third round in dummy, both defenders following (West playing the queen on the third round). When you exit with a club, West wins the ten, cashes the ♣Q. East follows with the jack, so it looks as if he started with ♣J62. West exits with a small spade and it's decision time. Your choice will only matter if the spade honors are split, but which of your honors do you play?

You have managed to delay the critical decision until trick ten, so plenty of information is available. In fact, you can build a fairly accurate picture of West's hand. His clubs and hearts are known exactly, and you can narrow the pointed suits down to two possibilities (he has followed to three rounds of diamonds and discarded one too). He must have started with one of these two hands:

♠ ? x x x		♠ ? x x
♥ x	*or*	♥ x
♦ Q x x x		♦ Q x x x x
♣ K Q 10 x		♣ K Q 10 x

So, having come this far, can you work out which spade honor West holds? Let's start by thinking about the play so far. The ♣K lead is consistent with either of these hands, but there is one clue to West's shape. As his first discard was a club, rather than a diamond, it seems more likely that he has the first, 4-1-4-4, distribution. With five diamonds, most defenders would see the long card in that suit as surplus to requirements, and throw it at the first opportunity. Having nailed down West's likely shape, does that help you with the important question — which spade honor does he have?

There is one slight inference from the early play. West's second discard was a diamond. With ♦Qxxx and ♠Axxx, it seems more likely that he would have parted with a spade, rather than weaken his tenuous diamond holding. However, if he had Qxxx in both pointed suits, surely he would be more inclined to throw a diamond, bearing in mind dummy's relative lengths in the two suits.

Before making a decision, think back to the bidding. Remember that West passed over your opening 1♥x bid. With ♠Axxx to go along with a singleton heart, ♦Qxxx and ♣KQ10x, is it not likely that West would have made what looks like an obvious takeout double of 1♥? The only explanation for his pass is that he does not have the ace of spades.

You therefore play the ♠J and this is the full hand:

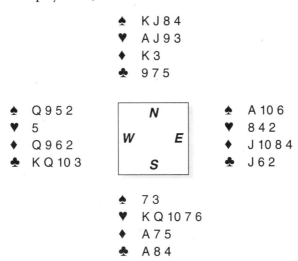

```
                  ♠   K J 8 4
                  ♥   A J 9 3
                  ♦   K 3
                  ♣   9 7 5

  ♠  Q 9 5 2          N          ♠  A 10 6
  ♥  5                            ♥  8 4 2
  ♦  Q 9 6 2     W       E        ♦  J 10 8 4
  ♣  K Q 10 3         S          ♣  J 6 2

                  ♠   7 3
                  ♥   K Q 10 7 6
                  ♦   A 7 5
                  ♣   A 8 4
```

On this hand, West's bidding (or lack of it) was the clear-cut clue. To realize this, you had to build a picture of his hand from the play. The next deal illustrates that information from the play can in itself be enlightening:

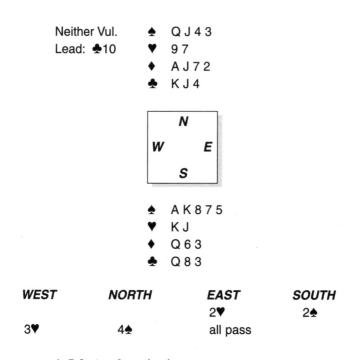

Neither Vul.
Lead: ♣10

♠ Q J 4 3
♥ 9 7
♦ A J 7 2
♣ K J 4

	N	
W		E
	S	

♠ A K 8 7 5
♥ K J
♦ Q 6 3
♣ Q 8 3

WEST	NORTH	EAST	SOUTH
		2♥	2♠
3♥	4♠	all pass	

1. 5-9 pts., 6-card suit

East wins ♣A and returns the ♥10. Do you play the king or the jack?

Does the bidding help? Not really, because in first seat most players would open a non-vulnerable weak two with either ♥Q10xxxx or ♥A10xxxx plus an outside ace. Similarly, the majority of responders tend to raise at the sniff of an oil rag in West's position. He would surely bid 3♥ with the ♦K and either ♥Axx or ♥Qxx.

So it's a guess? No, not even close. The question you should ask is why did West not lead a heart? Surely, holding ♥Qxx, he would lead his partner's suit more readily than a club from a suit headed by at best the ten. The only plausible explanation is that West has a dangerous heart holding from which to lead — ♥Axx.

Play the jack and be astounded if it loses to the queen.

As declarer, never lose sight of the fact that the defenders are not on your side. Of course, we all receive help from our opponents from time to time, but that is not their intention. All defenders make mistakes, but really good defensive players rarely go out of their way to assist declarer. It therefore stands to reason that if it appears they are trying to do so, you should be wary of 'Greeks bearing gifts'. By placing yourself in the defender's shoes you may be able to uncover his true motives.

With that reminder, how would you tackle the spades on this next hand?

```
E-W Vul.        ♠  J 5
Lead: ♦K        ♥  K J 9 3
                ♦  A 9 7 4 3
                ♣  8 4

              ┌─────────┐
              │    N    │
              │ W     E │
              │    S    │
              └─────────┘

                ♠  K 10
                ♥  A Q 10 7 4
                ♦  5 2
                ♣  A 10 5 2
```

WEST	NORTH	EAST	SOUTH
			1♥
pass	3♥	pass	4♥
all pass			

You take the ♦A and duck a club, West winning with the ♣7. The trump switch runs to dummy, and you play a club to the ace (West following with the queen), and ruff a club as West discards the ♠8. When you now exit with a diamond, East ruffs and returns the ♠6. Do you play the king or the ten?

There are two clues, both of which point to the same conclusion. First, consider the bidding. West has shown up with the ♦KQJ108, a doubleton ♣Q and at most two hearts. Even vulnerable, if he also has the ♠A he might have overcalled 2♦. A more significant clue comes from East's defense. Obviously, he could have discarded on the second diamond and allowed his partner to win the trick. There was no chance his partner would be endplayed, as he clearly has plenty of diamonds with which to exit. East also knows you have no winners on which to throw spades from either hand. So, why has he made the effort to gain the lead to play a spade?

Let us assume for the moment that your spades in hand are something like ♠K3. If that were the case, you would eventually ruff your club losers, draw trumps ending in dummy, and... then what? Yes, you would have no choice but to play East for the ♠A and lead a spade to the king. East doesn't know you have the ♠10, so from his perspective it looks as though you are fated to succeed if left to your own devices. Assuming East is a strong defender, you can be fairly sure that his play is designed purely to offer a losing option where one does not exist. On the evidence of both the bidding and the play you should rise with the ♠K and expect it to win. The full hand is:

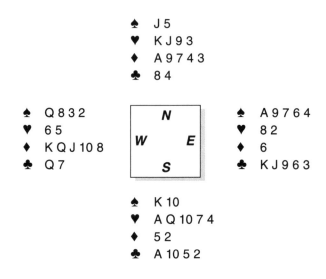

```
                    ♠  J 5
                    ♥  K J 9 3
                    ♦  A 9 7 4 3
                    ♣  8 4

♠ Q 8 3 2              N              ♠  A 9 7 6 4
♥ 6 5                                 ♥  8 2
♦ K Q J 10 8       W       E          ♦  6
♣ Q 7                 S               ♣  K J 9 6 3

                    ♠  K 10
                    ♥  A Q 10 7 4
                    ♦  5 2
                    ♣  A 10 5 2
```

As a final point, consider this layout:

Dummy
♣ K J x x

```
       N
   W       E
       S
```

Declarer
♣ 10 x x

You need two tricks from the suit. How do you rate your chances?

Your prospects range from poor to terrible: however, if West can be persuaded to lead the suit, you just need him to hold the queen. Bearing this position in mind, move around to West seat momentarily:

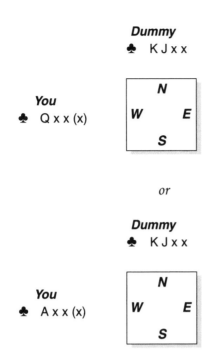

Dummy

♣ K J x x

You

♣ Q x x (x)

N
W E
S

or

Dummy

♣ K J x x

You

♣ A x x (x)

N
W E
S

Assuming you decide to lead this suit, which holding would you prefer? As we saw from the position above when declarer had ♣10xx, you are far more likely to give away a trick if you lead away from the queen. In a suit contract, a lead from the ace has the additional advantage that if partner has ♣ Qx (and declarer guesses wrong) you may also be able to give partner a ruff. If a defender voluntarily leads a suit in which you have a legitimate king-jack guess (e.g. KJxx opposite xx) you should be inclined to place him with the ace rather than the queen.

- King-jack positions come in various guises.

- Depending on which cards are hidden and which are in dummy, it may or may not be obvious to the defenders that you *have* a king-jack guess.

- An early lead towards a king-jack combination in dummy will often encourage West to play the ace if he has it.

- You should generally delay the decision in a 'guess' suit, since a count of the defenders' distribution and/or high-card points will often enable you to guess correctly.

- If a good defender gives you a king-jack guess when one does not legitimately exist, assume that playing the king (which you would have to do without his help) is the winning play.

- If a good defender voluntarily leads through dummy's king-jack early in the play, he is much more likely to have the ace than the queen.

CHAPTER 10

Using the Defenders' Cards to Get a Count

W e have repeatedly seen how much easier things are when you know the shape of the defensive hands. A primary source of distributional information is noting whether an opponent follows suit or discards when you play off winners. Data collected in this way is guaranteed — if a defender discards on the third round of a suit, you can be sure he started with a doubleton. Knowledge of the closed hands gleaned from the bidding can be nearly as reliable. For example, a 1NT opener will usually have a balanced hand within a stated point range. Similarly, if a player passes as dealer you can assume he has fewer than thirteen high card points.

Inferences based on the defenders' carding are less reliable. However, there are situations in which you can be reasonably sure their signals are truthful. For example, if an opponent leads the lowest outstanding card in a suit and their agreed method is to lead fourth-highest, he will seldom have a five-card suit. Similarly, if the leader's partner encourages or shows an even number of cards by playing high-low, he will rarely have three small cards in the suit. The difficulty is that defenders are not obliged to signal honestly. Having said that, they usually have to do so if there is a significant risk of misleading their partner, and it is this dilemma that you must exploit as declarer.

Whenever you play several boards against a pair, it is easy enough to test the accuracy of their signalling. For example, let's say you become declarer on an early board. You have eleven top tricks in a dull 4♠ contract and you have a side suit of ♣ KQx in dummy opposite ♣ Axx. At trick two, lead towards the ♣ KQx to see whether the defenders signal count. When the hand is over, surreptitiously check whether they signalled honestly. This information may come in handy later, when it really matters.

Most competent defenders signal honestly early in the hand. Equally, most do not signal in the later play. With that hint, how would you approach this first hand?

Neither Vul.   ♠ J 7
Lead: ♣6   ♥ J 6 4 3
             ♦ K Q 10 3
             ♣ Q 8 4

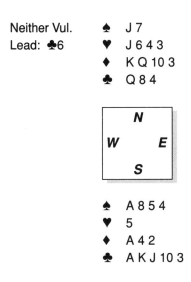

♠ A 8 5 4
♥ 5
♦ A 4 2
♣ A K J 10 3

WEST	NORTH	EAST	SOUTH
		pass	1♣
pass	1♦	1♥	1♠
2♥	3♣	pass	5♣
all pass			

You win the first trick in hand with the ♣10. What now? Most players would duck a spade, planning to win the trump return, play the ♠A and ruff a spade before crossing back to hand to draw the last trump. A correct diamond guess then disposes of the remaining spade loser. Can you see a way to improve your chances?

With a little foresight you can make your task much easier. At trick two, try the effect of leading a diamond to the king. West plays the ♦8 and East the ♦9. You then follow the same line of play as above, but now, when it comes to guessing the diamonds, you will have no problem picking up ♦J865 in the West hand since both defenders helpfully showed an even number of cards in the suit at trick two. 'They might not signal accurately, though,' you say. This is true, but unlikely. West is almost sure to play a true card in case your diamond is a singleton. In that case, it is vital for him to give an accurate count so that East knows to take his ace. If, instead, you ruff the spade loser and draw trumps before touching diamonds, you will be able to tell nothing from how the defenders follow to the first two rounds of diamonds. By then, they will both be aware of the situation, and know that signalling will only help you, not them.

On the last hand, a defensive signal helped you to determine the distribution of the key suit. On the next deal, the opponents tip off the position of a high card. If you're feeling wide awake, cover the East-West hands and play declarer's cards.

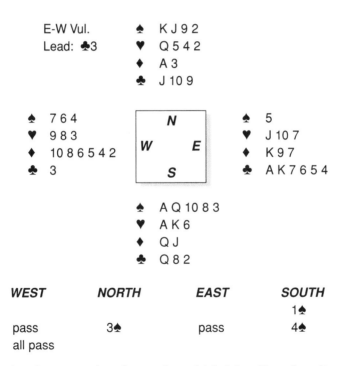

```
E-W Vul.        ♠  K J 9 2
Lead: ♣3        ♥  Q 5 4 2
                ♦  A 3
                ♣  J 10 9

    ♠  7 6 4         N          ♠  5
    ♥  9 8 3                    ♥  J 10 7
    ♦  10 8 6 5 4 2  W     E    ♦  K 9 7
    ♣  3             S          ♣  A K 7 6 5 4

                ♠  A Q 10 8 3
                ♥  A K 6
                ♦  Q J
                ♣  Q 8 2
```

WEST	NORTH	EAST	SOUTH
			1♠
pass	3♠	pass	4♠
all pass			

East wins the ♣K, cashes the ace (on which West discards a diamond) and leads the ♣4 for West to ruff. A diamond is returned and you have reached the decision point. Do you finesse?

Vacant Spaces Theory suggests that West is more likely to have the ♦K since he has twelve non-clubs to East's seven — 63%. Those seem like pretty good odds, don't they? Rather than blindly follow such odds though, you should trust your opponents to defend in a sane manner. If West has the ♦K, will he really switch to the suit when you may have the unsupported queen?

Also ask yourself why East returned the four of clubs, a clear suit-preference signal for a diamond, when you know he had a choice of clubs — 7, 6, 5 or 4. Could this be a deceptive signal by East? Surely not, for if West has the ♦KJ, a diamond switch may just give away a trick, and can never gain. You can be sure that the only time a competent East will signal for a diamond is when he has the king. You should rely on East's signal, and West's sanity, and rise with the ♦A. Having cashed five rounds of spades, you can play on hearts. You will make ten tricks if hearts break 3-3 or via a squeeze (whenever either defender started with the ♦K and at least four hearts).

There are many situations in which you can force competent defenders to signal accurately. Take the East cards on this deal:

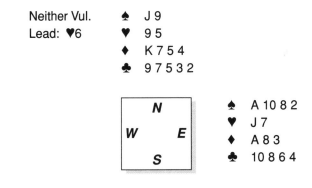

```
Neither Vul.        ♠  J 9
Lead: ♥6            ♥  9 5
                    ♦  K 7 5 4
                    ♣  9 7 5 3 2

                              ♠  A 10 8 2
         N                    ♥  J 7
    W         E               ♦  A 8 3
         S                    ♣  10 8 6 4
```

WEST	NORTH	EAST	SOUTH
			2♣
pass	2♦	pass	2NT
pass	3NT	all pass	

Your ♥J loses to the king at Trick 1 and declarer leads the ♦Q. West plays the ♦2 and you duck. Now declarer leads the ♦J and partner follows with the ♦6. Do you win or duck?

With no obvious entry to dummy, partner's low-high (showing an odd number of diamonds) tells you to duck again so that declarer cannot make a third diamond trick. If, instead, partner played high-low (to show an even number), you would win the second diamond. If partner has four then declarer is entitled to only one diamond trick, while if declarer has a 4-4 diamond fit you cannot prevent him from making three tricks in the suit.

Now move around to the South seat and consider how you should play this next hand:

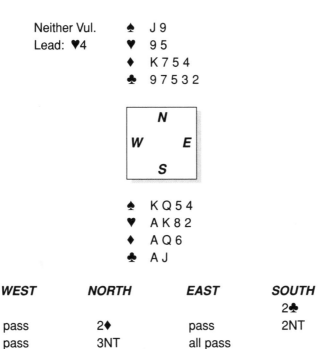

Neither Vul.	♠	J 9
Lead: ♥4	♥	9 5
	♦	K 7 5 4
	♣	9 7 5 3 2

	♠	K Q 5 4
	♥	A K 8 2
	♦	A Q 6
	♣	A J

WEST	NORTH	EAST	SOUTH
			2♣
pass	2♦	pass	2NT
pass	3NT	all pass	

The opening lead runs to East's ♥J and your ♥K. Despite 27 combined high card points, you have only six top tricks; two more can be developed in spades. You have two chances for a ninth trick — a 3-3 diamond break or a finesse against the ♠10. However, there is no safe way to combine both chances.

One possible line of play is to knock out the ♠A and then play for a 3-3 diamond break. Testing diamonds first is not an option — if they do not break, you will not have enough entries to take a spade finesse and establish three tricks in the suit without setting up five tricks for the defense. The other option is to take an immediate finesse against the ♠10. If that wins then you can knock out the ♠A and claim nine tricks. However, if East has the ♠10 and West the ♠A, the defense will establish and cash three heart tricks and you will go down even if diamonds break. Can you improve on these two options?

It seems that you have to guess, but perhaps you can combine your chances after all. Try the effect of leading the ♦Q at trick two. Both defenders are likely to give an accurate count signal in case their partner has the ♦A. If they both follow with a low diamond, you should play on the assumption that diamonds are breaking. You are hoping the hand is:

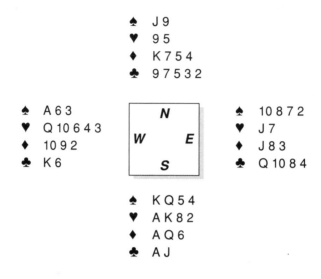

If both defenders play fairly high diamonds (one probably signalling a doubleton, the other four) then you should play a spade to the nine at trick three.

There are several situations in which the defenders must signal accurately in the early play. If you need to discover how a particular suit lies, put yourself mentally in a defender's seat and ask what you would do in various situations. On the hand above, consider how you would signal if declarer led the ♦A from his hand instead of the ♦Q — surely, both defenders should play low no matter what their holdings. Yes, the defenders against you *may* signal accurately, but they have no real reason to do so. But when you lead the queen, competent defenders almost *have* to tell you what you need to know.

LESSONS FROM THIS CHAPTER

- The opening lead and early signals are usually honest and you can treat information gained from these cards as reliable.

- If you need the defenders to tell you how a suit is breaking, do not wait to play the suit until they know enough not to signal.

- In a long match, test the honesty of your opponents' signals at an early stage.

- Watch your opponents' suit-preference signals to locate missing high cards.

- Gauge the authenticity of information by considering the problem from the defender's point of view. If you decide that he cannot afford to play a deceptive card for fear that his partner will do the wrong thing, then treat the information as reliable

CHAPTER 11

Bringing It All Together as Declarer

Throughout Section 2 of this book we have looked at numerous situations in which counting will help your declarer play. You have seen the techniques your expert opponents use against you. In this final chapter on declarer play, we see experts playing hands that, at first glance, appear more difficult than those tackled so far.

Your first reaction to most of these hands will quite likely be 'I could never do that.' However, if you work carefully through the explanation of each deal, you will realize that the reasoning behind the solutions found at the table is based on little more than counting to thirteen.

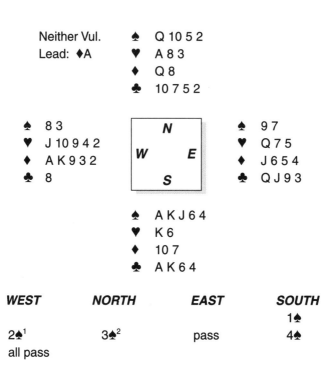

Neither Vul.
Lead: ♦A

♠ Q 10 5 2
♥ A 8 3
♦ Q 8
♣ 10 7 5 2

♠ 8 3
♥ J 10 9 4 2
♦ A K 9 3 2
♣ 8

♠ 9 7
♥ Q 7 5
♦ J 6 5 4
♣ Q J 9 3

♠ A K J 6 4
♥ K 6
♦ 10 7
♣ A K 6 4

WEST	NORTH	EAST	SOUTH
			1♠
2♠[1]	3♠[2]	pass	4♠
all pass			

1. Hearts and a minor
2. Less than a limit raise.

West led the ♦AK and switched to the ♥J. Declarer won in hand, drew trumps with the ♠AK, played a heart to the ace, and ruffed dummy's last heart. Can you see what he did next, and why?

Twelve of West's cards were known — ten cards in the red suits and two spades. Hoping that West's thirteenth card was a club higher than the three, declarer led a low club from hand. When West played the ♣8 declarer *ducked*, giving East a choice of poisons. As allowing the ♣8 to hold would leave West forced to concede a ruff and discard, East overtook with the ♣9 and returned a hopeful ♣3. Knowing that West had no more clubs, declarer played low and collected three club tricks to go with seven from the majors.

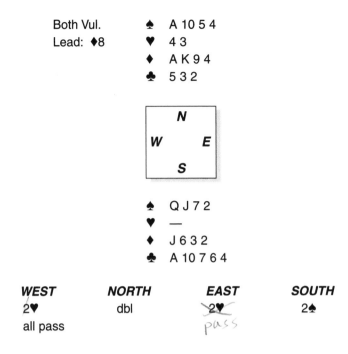

Both Vul. ♠ A 10 5 4
Lead: ♦8 ♥ 4 3
          ♦ A K 9 4
          ♣ 5 3 2

          N
        W   E
          S

          ♠ Q J 7 2
          ♥ —
          ♦ J 6 3 2
          ♣ A 10 7 6 4

WEST	NORTH	EAST	SOUTH
2♥	dbl	~~2♥~~	2♠
all pass		*pass*	

A count of the preemptor's hand can sometimes allow you to overcome an adverse ruff. As an aside, it is worth noting that on most occasions when a defender makes a preemptive bid and then leads a different side suit, the lead will be a singleton.

Here, you win the opening lead with the ♦A and immediately ruff a heart. The ♠Q holds the next trick and a spade to the ten wins as both defenders follow, so you ruff dummy's second heart with your final trump.

You can count nine sure tricks — six trumps (including two heart ruffs), two diamonds and the ♣A. Your first shot at a tenth trick is to lead a diamond towards dummy. If West discards, you will be able to win the ♦K, draw the last trump and lead up to the ♦J to make the hand.

However, West is alert to this ruse. He ruffs the diamond and leads the ♥Q. It's time to reconstruct the defenders' hands. West started with three spades, probably seven hearts, one diamond and therefore two clubs. This is only an inferential count since hearts could be 8-3, but there is no way to find out for certain so you have to make an 'educated guess'. If you are correct that West was 3-7-1-2, then East's shape was 2-4-4-3. That leaves these cards:

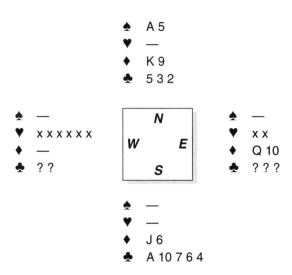

The 'x' means that the value of the card is irrelevant, and the '?' that it may be an unknown high card. The vital information that your count of the hand provides is that East holds the long club. Can you see a way to use that information to bring home your contract?

You must ruff the heart in dummy and duck a club. Regardless of which defender wins the club trick, you ruff the heart return with dummy's last trump, cash the ♣A, and at Trick 11 exit with a third round of clubs which only East will be able to win. Since East's last two cards are known to be the ♦Q10, he will be unable to prevent you from scoring your tenth trick with the ♦J.

The squeeze is often considered to be the exclusive domain of experts, but as Victor Mollo's Rueful Rabbit often pointed out, if you just cash your winners, defenders frequently throw the wrong card. Of course, when a legitimate squeeze operates, it doesn't matter which card the defender throws. The moral of the Rabbit's tale though, is that it is not necessary to foresee the ending in order to execute a squeeze. It is important, however, as we saw in an earlier chapter, to know which 'loser' is in fact a winner once the defender has been squeezed. On the next deal, declarer had only to cash his winners in the right order, and to do that he had to count.

(see hand at the top of the next page)

South's Key Card Blackwood response showed two key cards and the trump queen, and North's 5NT bid was a grand slam try confirming possession of the missing key cards. South decided that his sixth spade, coupled with the likelihood of benefiting from the information provided by the preempt, was enough to attempt the grand slam.

N-S Vul. ♠ K J 4
Lead: ♣K ♥ 6 5 4 3
          ♦ A K J 5 2
          ♣ A

♠ 7 6 2   ♠ 3
♥ 10   ♥ Q J 9 8 7 2
♦ 7 6   ♦ Q 9 8
♣ K Q J 10 9 5 2   ♣ 7 6 3

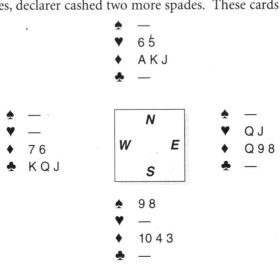

          ♠ A Q 10 9 8 5
          ♥ A K
          ♦ 10 4 3
          ♣ 8 4

WEST	NORTH	EAST	SOUTH
			1♠
4♣	4NT	pass	5♠
pass	5NT	pass	7♠
all pass			

Declarer won the ♣A, overtook the ♠K, ruffed his second club with the ♠J and drew trumps. He now knew at least ten of West's cards — seven clubs and three spades. To gather more information, he cashed the ♥AK. When West discarded on the second heart, East was marked with six hearts and at least three diamonds. Obviously, there was little point in taking a diamond finesse — if West had the ♦Q, it would fall when the ♦AK were played later. Following general principles, declarer cashed two more spades. These cards remained:

          ♠ —
          ♥ 6 5
          ♦ A K J
          ♣ —

♠ —   ♠ —
♥ —   ♥ Q J
♦ 7 6   ♦ Q 9 8
♣ K Q J   ♣ —

          ♠ 9 8
          ♥ —
          ♦ 10 4 3
          ♣ —

The ♦J was thrown from dummy on the penultimate trump, but what could East discard? If he threw a heart, declarer would play a diamond to the table and ruff the ♥5 to set up the last heart in dummy. If East threw a diamond, the ♦AK would be cashed and a heart ruff would enable declarer to return to the good ♦10 in hand.

Preemptive bids are often very revealing when the bidder's side does not buy the contract. On the next deal, Australian international Andrew Reiner made good use of the information provided by the defensive bidding. It was enough to ensure his team's victory in the 1977 Australian Teams Championships.

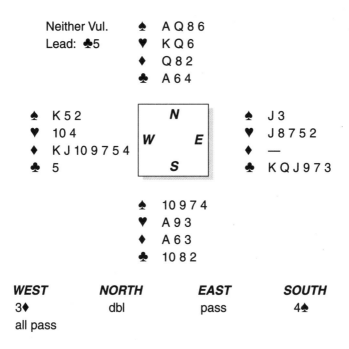

Neither Vul.	♠	A Q 8 6
Lead: ♣5	♥	K Q 6
	♦	Q 8 2
	♣	A 6 4

West:
♠ K 5 2
♥ 10 4
♦ K J 10 9 7 5 4
♣ 5

East:
♠ J 3
♥ J 8 7 5 2
♦ —
♣ K Q J 9 7 3

South:
♠ 10 9 7 4
♥ A 9 3
♦ A 6 3
♣ 10 8 2

WEST	NORTH	EAST	SOUTH
3♦	dbl	pass	4♠
all pass			

The VuGraph commentators were confidently predicting defeat, but Reiner demonstrated that ten tricks were possible if you could 'see' the defenders' hands. Reasoning that when a preemptive bidder leads another side suit it is usually a singleton, he rose with dummy's ♣A at trick one. A heart to the ace was followed by a spade to the queen. The ♠A and the top hearts came next. When West discarded on the third round of hearts, declarer was sure his original shape had been 3-2-7-1.

Armed with this information, Reiner exited with a club to East. After taking his two club tricks, East had to concede a ruff and discard, allowing declarer to dispose of a diamond loser. West was then endplayed with his trump winner to lead away from the ♦K. You may also have noticed that declarer could have reversed the order of these endplays by exiting with a third trump after having cashed the hearts. After the forced diamond return away from the king, he would cash his other diamond winner and then endplay either opponent to concede a ruff and discard.

Throughout this section on declarer play, we have seen many hands on which declarer took advantage of the opponents' bidding, but we finish with the case of a dog that *didn't* bark. This deal also originated Down Under, where it was beautifully played by Warren Lazer of Sydney at the 1998 Australian Summer Nationals. The hand provides a graphic illustration of how experts find stratagems that may seem astounding to most players. Having travelled this far with us on the journey towards understanding the logic behind the expert's thinking, we hope you now consider such poetry within reach.

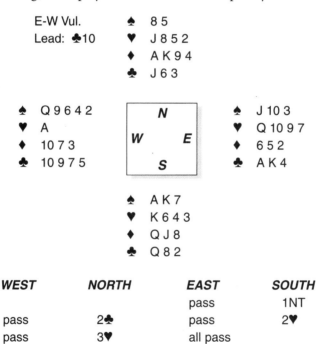

```
                    E-W Vul.      ♠  8 5
                    Lead: ♣10     ♥  J 8 5 2
                                  ♦  A K 9 4
                                  ♣  J 6 3

        ♠  Q 9 6 4 2          N            ♠  J 10 3
        ♥  A                               ♥  Q 10 9 7
        ♦  10 7 3        W          E       ♦  6 5 2
        ♣  10 9 7 5          S            ♣  A K 4

                                  ♠  A K 7
                                  ♥  K 6 4 3
                                  ♦  Q J 8
                                  ♣  Q 8 2
```

WEST	NORTH	EAST	SOUTH
		pass	1NT
pass	2♣	pass	2♥
pass	3♥	all pass	

Opposite a 15-17 notrump, North's decision not to bid game showed a pessimism that turned out to be correct. West fired away with a club and East played ace, king and a third round to declarer's queen. Since East passed as dealer, declarer figured West was odds-on to have the ♥A, and so he played a small trump from hand at trick four.

When West played the ace on thin air, the trump position became clear.

Declarer won the spade switch and continued spades himself, ruffing the third round. Three rounds of diamonds followed to produce this ending:

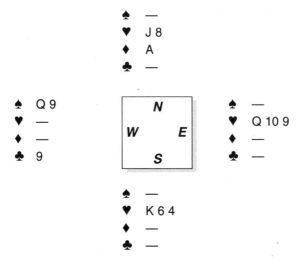

Declarer led the ♦A from dummy and, as expected, East was forced to ruff. Lazer *underruffed,* leaving East to lead away from the ♥Q at trick twelve. Spectacular? For sure. Impossible for mere mortals to find? Not if they can count to thirteen.

Counting on Defense

CHAPTER 12

Signalling on Defense

As beginners, we are all taught to play a high card to tell partner we like a suit and a low one to say we don't — in other words, to signal our 'attitude' to the suit. This is an easy signalling method to understand. It is also ideal for novices as it means they can take their winners and wait for partner to tell them what to do next. Unfortunately, if high to encourage and low to discourage is the only signal in your arsenal, you will not be able to solve many defensive problems. To appreciate this, you only have to go to your local club, where you will often hear a defender make a comment such as, 'but you told me to lead a club.' Such recriminations occur because, on the hand in question, a club was not the right thing to lead.

The attitude signal is only one of the methods used by good defenders. In the course of this chapter we are going to discuss a signalling system involving the three major types of signal — attitude, count and suit-preference. To optimize your defense, you will need to employ a combination of these. Our first hand illustrates one reason why playing only attitude signals does not work:

```
Neither Vul.        ♠  6 5 3 2
Lead: ♥K           ♥  A J 4
                    ♦  Q 10 6
                    ♣  Q 10 6

You
♠  K 4
♥  K Q 10 8 3            N
♦  9 7 3          W           E
♣  K 8 4                S
```

WEST	NORTH	EAST	SOUTH
1♥	pass	3♠[1]	4♠
dbl	all pass		

1. Splinter in support of hearts

Dummy's ♥A wins Trick 1 as partner plays the ♥7 (high-low to show an even number) and South follows with the ♥5. Declarer plays a spade to his ace, and a second spade to your king on which partner discards the ♥6. What do you play now?

Many players would automatically switch to a diamond. Why? Because leading your high heart (which you know declarer will ruff) establishes dummy's jack, and leading away from the ♣K looks too dangerous. However, think about partner's signal. 'What signal?', you may ask.

It is time to examine the basic philosophy behind defensive signalling. The underlying principle of effective defense is not that one member of the partnership tells the other what to lead or switch to. After all, why should East, looking at only his thirteen cards and dummy, know what to do any more than West? To operate efficiently as a partnership, one defender (in this case, East) must tell the other about his hand. West will then effectively be able to 'see' both defensive hands and should be able to work out what to do. Of course, this requires the defenders to put in some effort since they must count points and distribution, but it is the only way to defend accurately on a consistent basis. So, what about East's signal (or apparent lack of one) on the hand above? As West, what do you know about the hand?

East showed the values for a raise to game, so he must have some high-card points. If he had something like the ♦AK, would he not encourage diamonds (or discourage clubs)? If that happened, you could play a diamond to his king and he would return a club, establishing your four defensive tricks. Could it be that East could not afford to discard from either minor? Perhaps, but he could have given a suit-preference signal with either the ♥9 or the ♥2, and he didn't do that either — he played the middle card of his remaining hearts. Why is partner being so obtuse? The answer is that he is actually being very helpful. The message is coming across loud and clear — he does not know which minor you should switch to. The implication is that he has similar holdings in both suits, and with that information you can work out what to play.

Having decided that partner has the values for game (let's say about ten points) and similar minor-suit holdings, you can deduce that he must have the ace-jack of both minors. Once you come to that conclusion, the club switch is obvious. Indeed, to ensure that partner cannot go wrong, you should play the ♣K and then a second club. This is the full hand:

```
                    ♠   6 5 3 2
                    ♥   A J 4
                    ♦   Q 10 6
                    ♣   Q 10 6

   ♠   K 4              N          ♠   7
   ♥   K Q 10 8 3                  ♥   9 7 6 2
   ♦   9 7 3       W       E       ♦   A J 5 2
   ♣   K 8 4            S          ♣   A J 7 3

                    ♠   A Q J 10 9 8
                    ♥   5
                    ♦   K 8 4
                    ♣   9 5 2
```

Playing a heart or a diamond collects +300. A club switch gets you +500 as East exits with a heart once you have taken your three club tricks. Now declarer must now lose a second red-suit trick in addition to the ♦A.

Note that if East-West are playing Lavinthal, Revolving, Odd-Even, or some other method of signalling in which a discard tells partner which minor to switch to, then East must guess which suit to ask for. Half the time he will guess wrong as he has no clue which is better. Any method of signalling which requires one partner to make the decision for both players is clearly flawed.

On this hand, a combination of signals led you to the optimum defense. The signalling method we are going to recommend here is based primarily on count, with a liberal sprinkling of attitude and suit-preference as the situation demands. We'll begin with a brief look at each of the primary signalling tools available to the defenders.

It is impossible to defend consistently well without being able to count the shape of declarer's (and thus partner's) hand. For this reason, it is count (or distributional) signals that form the backbone of sound partnership defense.

If the opening leader's partner does not need to try to win Trick 1, the most important information he can give his partner is how many cards he has in the suit led. (There are exceptions to this, but we shall discuss them later.) The same is true when following suit early in the hand.

When you are defending, the opponents are bound to have provided you with information during the bidding. This will usually enable you to place most of the high cards, and the early play will often complete this job. What defenders most need to know is the distribution of the hidden hands. Whether you decide to play your count signals in standard fashion (high-low to show an even number of cards in the suit) or upside-down (high-low to show an odd number) doesn't really matter. Use the method with which both you and your partner feel most comfortable. You do not want to expend a great deal of mental energy on the basic counting processes. If you are used to seeing a high-low and automatically knowing it shows an even number, do not switch just for the sake of being in fashion (or appearing clever).

The next deal illustrates how count signals can ensure the defenders take all of the tricks due to them:

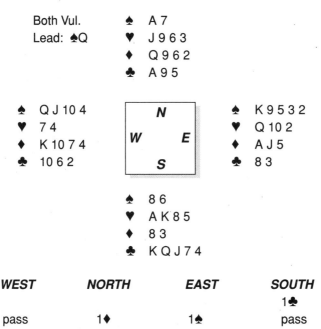

```
                  Both Vul.        ♠  A 7
                  Lead: ♠Q         ♥  J 9 6 3
                                   ♦  Q 9 6 2
                                   ♣  A 9 5

         ♠  Q J 10 4          N            ♠  K 9 5 3 2
         ♥  7 4                             ♥  Q 10 2
         ♦  K 10 7 4      W       E         ♦  A J 5
         ♣  10 6 2            S             ♣  8 3

                                   ♠  8 6
                                   ♥  A K 8 5
                                   ♦  8 3
                                   ♣  K Q J 7 4
```

WEST	NORTH	EAST	SOUTH
			1♣
pass	1♦	1♠	pass
3♠	dbl	pass	4♥
all pass			

Dummy's ♠A wins trick one as East follows with the ♠2. Declarer cashes the ♥AK and then plays the ♣AKQ, hoping the defender with the outstanding trump will have to follow to three clubs. However, East ruffs the third club.

Think about the problem from East's perspective. If the defense is to have any hope of beating the contract, West must have the ♦K. However, East cannot tell how many spades his partner had to begin with. If he had five, then South is now void and the defenders need to take three diamond tricks. If West had only four spades, then declarer has two diamonds and a spade to lose. In either case, it is safe for East to lead a diamond to West's king: he must then rely on West to tell him what to do.

If West returns a second diamond, East should cash the third diamond and expect it to stand up. Why? Because it is West who has all the necessary information. East played the ♠2 (lowest from an odd number) at trick one, telling his partner that he had only five spades. If there is a spade trick to cash, then it is up to West to take it. On the actual hand, West must win the ♦K and cash the ♠J before leading the second diamond. Basic count signalling enables the defenders to make the four tricks they are due, irrespective of whether South's shape is 2-4-2-5 or 1-4-3-5.

If East-West were playing only attitude signals, East would play a high spade at trick one to show the king and West would not know whether there was a spade trick to be taken. He would win the ♦K and return a diamond and East would be left to guess whether to try to cash the ♦A or the ♠K. Attitude signals are clearly useless here — what should be a simple defensive problem would be reduced to a guess. East would not make a vulnerable overcall on ♠98532, so West already knows who has the king. The information West needs is whether East's spades are ♠K9532 or ♠K98532.

Despite our previous comments, though, there are situations in which the attitude signal is a vital weapon. Once again, you can choose to play your attitude signals in the standard way (high to encourage) or upside-down. We recommend that you use attitude signals only on the lead of an ace in cash-out situations against high-level contracts and sacrifices. If partner leads an ace against a contract at the four-level or below, you should assume he has ace-king and encourage holding the queen (or a doubleton against a suit contract), but otherwise you should discourage. When you are defending a high-level contract (five-level or above) partner will be more inclined to lead an unsupported ace, so now you should only play an encouraging card if you have the king.

The objective of leading an honor is to score tricks immediately or to establish winners. We suggest that your choice of lead from an honor sequence should depend on the signal you want to see. This means that you have a choice when leading from a suit headed by ace-king. Lead the ace from holdings such as AKx and partner will tell you whether or not he likes the suit. With AKxxx or AKQx, lead the king and partner will give count so that you can tell how many tricks you can cash. This allows you to combine the benefits of attitude and count signalling.

You can also agree to similar methods when leading from king-queen. For example, if you decide to lead from KQx or KQ10x, lead the queen and partner will encourage with the ace or jack. From KQJxx, lead the king and partner will give count.

Discarding methods are another matter entirely, and here we recommend that you adopt a different type of attitude signal. An efficient method is to treat all discards as discouraging, denying interest in the suit thrown. The basic philosophy is that you throw from a suit in which you do not have anything. One reason for this is that sometimes you will not be dealt a card which is 'obviously high' or 'obviously low' (or the right spot for an odd-even signal), or you will not be able to afford to throw a card carrying the message you want to send.

Partner will usually have a choice of only two suits to switch to, but there are situations when there are three possible suits partner might play. Let's say partner is cashing spades and you have a diamond honor. Playing our discarding method, if you throw a heart and a club, partner will know where your honor is. Alternatively, if the situation is similar to that in the first hand above, when you had honors in both minors, you can throw two hearts; again, partner will know what you have and should be able to work out which switch to make.

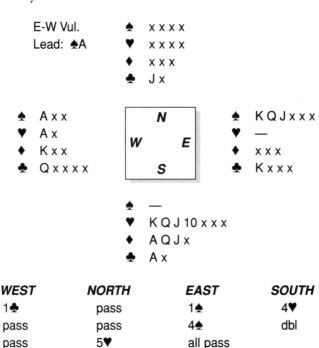

E-W Vul.
Lead: ♠A

♠ x x x x
♥ x x x x
♦ x x x
♣ J x

♠ A x x
♥ A x
♦ K x x
♣ Q x x x x

N
W E
S

♠ K Q J x x x
♥ —
♦ x x x
♣ K x x x

♠ —
♥ K Q J 10 x x x
♦ A Q J x
♣ A x

WEST	NORTH	EAST	SOUTH
1♣	pass	1♠	4♥
pass	pass	4♠	dbl
pass	5♥	all pass	

Declarer ruffs the opening ♠A lead and plays the ♥K. West takes his ace and East discards... what?

Playing standard attitude discards, East will usually have either a low diamond or a high club to throw. No problem; either signal tells West he should play a club and the contract will go down. What if you are dealt ♦987 and ♣K432, though? Perhaps partner can work out that the ♦7 is a low card or that the ♣4 is a high one, but sometimes he won't be able to and, as a result, will do something that allows the contract to make.

'This is why I prefer upside-down signals,' you say. Really? That's why we intentionally marked the small cards as 'x' in the diagram. If you are playing upside-down signals, East has ♦432 and ♣K987. Again, West *might* get it right, but often he will not. No, upside-down signals aren't the answer, either.

'So partner should duck the first heart so that he can see if I play high-low,' you say. Well, that doesn't seem to work either. Instead of a second heart, declarer plays the ♦A and then the ♦Q — although West wins the ♦K and switches to a club, it's all too late. West finds himself ruffing the fourth round of diamonds with his ace of trumps as declarer discards dummy's club loser.

The simple answer is for East to be able to discard any diamond to show a club honor (or vice versa). If East has either an honor in both minors or an honor in neither, he discards a spade. West will be able to tell from the bidding, and his own hand, which it is. He will then always find a winning defense if one exists. We apologize if this concept of throwing losers and keeping winners seems too simple. Think about it, though — how often have you seen someone signal with a card they cannot afford for a suit they don't really want?

The third signalling weapon in the defenders' armory is the suit-preference signal. Also called McKenney or Lavinthal signals, many players think of these only as discarding signals. Suit-preference signals can be useful when leading or following suit, though. Often, count and attitude in the suit being played are either obvious or irrelevant, but the order in which you play your small cards can still convey a useful message. This is the simplest and most common suit-preference situation, with which everyone is familiar:

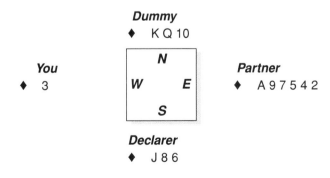

Dummy
♦ K Q 10

You
♦   3

N
W   E
S

Partner
♦ A 9 7 5 4 2

Declarer
♦   J 8 6

You are defending a heart contract and this is the diamond suit. Partner leads the ♦3 at trick one, so you win your ace and give him a ruff. Clearly, which diamond you play is irrelevant since the ♦97542 are effectively equal. You therefore select the diamond that tells partner how to get you in for a second ruff. If you want partner to switch to spades, you return the ♦9 (the high card suggests an entry in the higher of the other two suits). If you want a club back, you tell partner with the ♦2. With no preference, you return a middle card, the ♦5.

Suit-preference signals based on this principle can be utilized in many less obvious situations. For example, when declarer is cashing winners in a suit there is usually no need for you to signal count — the chances are that you are going to show out anyway. It is much more efficient to use such opportunities to send partner a useful message. The most likely information you will want to impart relates to your holdings in the other two suits. Let's say you are defending a heart contract and this is the diamond suit:

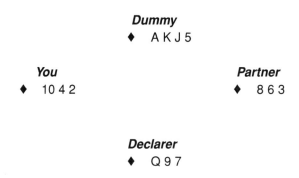

Dummy

♦ A K J 5

You

♦ 10 4 2

Partner

♦ 8 6 3

Declarer

♦ Q 9 7

Declarer cashes the queen and then crosses to dummy, presumably to cash his winners. Do you think there is any need for either defender to signal their length? No. If you want to send a suit-preference signal though, it is easy to do so. If a defender plays his cards upwards, this should suggest interest in clubs (the lower of the remaining suits). Playing the cards from the top would show something in spades. Starting with the middle card (and then playing the other two in either order) would show no particular message to send.

This is a situation that occurs time and time again for defenders, yet remarkably few of them take advantage of it. Another common position where you can, if you wish, seize the opportunity for a suit-preference signal is when declarer is drawing trumps. Often you and your partner will simply be following routinely with small cards; if signalling length is irrelevant, and you cannot possibly want a ruff, it makes sense to signal suit-preference here too.

With all this in mind, try covering the West and South cards and treating the next deal as a defensive problem from the East seat.

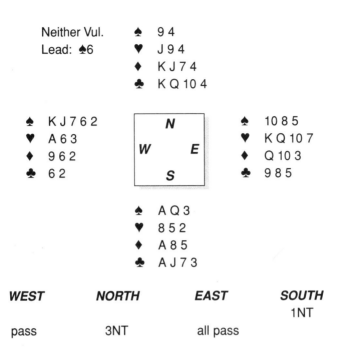

Neither Vul.
Lead: ♠6

	♠	9 4
	♥	J 9 4
	♦	K J 7 4
	♣	K Q 10 4

♠ K J 7 6 2		♠ 10 8 5
♥ A 6 3		♥ K Q 10 7
♦ 9 6 2		♦ Q 10 3
♣ 6 2		♣ 9 8 5

	♠	A Q 3
	♥	8 5 2
	♦	A 8 5
	♣	A J 7 3

WEST	NORTH	EAST	SOUTH
			1NT
pass	3NT	all pass	

Declarer takes your ♠10 with the queen, cashes the ♦A and plays the ♦8 to dummy's jack. You win the ♦Q. What now?

Most players would continue spades without considering any alternative. Looking at the full hand though, it is clear you must play a heart. South's 1NT opening showed 15-17 HCP, so you know partner has 6-8 HCP. A spade continuation will be right if he has led from ♠AJxxx. When his high cards are the ♠K and the ♥A, as here, it will not. How can you tell?

Do you care how many diamonds partner has? Of course not. Instead of conveying this useless message you would rather he gave you information that will help solve your actual problem. If West plays his highest diamond at every opportunity — the ♦9 then the ♦6 — that tells you that he likes the higher of the two possible suits (clubs being irrelevant because of dummy's holding) and you should return a spade expecting him to cash four tricks in the suit. If, instead, he follows with the ♦2 then the ♦6, this suggests something in the lower suit (i.e. hearts) and you should switch to a heart hoping to cash four tricks in that suit.

Can you say with confidence that you and your regular partner would have beaten this contract? Such defense demands significant partnership cooperation and understanding, and illustrates why expert defenders beat many more contracts than do less experienced pairs.

Defending a suit contract, there is considerable scope for signalling while trumps are being drawn. With two or three small trumps, when it is clear that declarer will draw them all, you can send a suit-preference signal by the order in which you follow suit. The situation is different if partner is going to gain the lead while you still have trumps. It is then normal for a high-low in trumps to tell partner that you want to ruff something. You echo (play high-low) to confirm that you have a third trump or, as in this next example, that you are able to ruff. Cover the West and South cards and take East's seat if you feel so inclined.

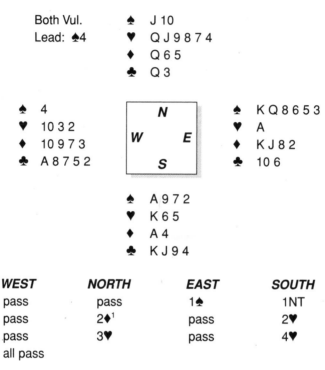

Both Vul.
Lead: ♠4

North:
♠ J 10
♥ Q J 9 8 7 4
♦ Q 6 5
♣ Q 3

West:
♠ 4
♥ 10 3 2
♦ 10 9 7 3
♣ A 8 7 5 2

East:
♠ K Q 8 6 5 3
♥ A
♦ K J 8 2
♣ 10 6

South:
♠ A 9 7 2
♥ K 6 5
♦ A 4
♣ K J 9 4

WEST	NORTH	EAST	SOUTH
pass	pass	1♠	1NT
pass	2♦[1]	pass	2♥
pass	3♥	pass	4♥
all pass			

1. Transfer

Partner leads the ♠4 and your ♠Q loses to South's ace. Declarer leads a heart to the queen and West signals with the ♥10 as you win the ace. What now?

Partner's ♥10 is obviously not a singleton so it must be the start of a high-low. The message must be that he can ruff the next spade, and therefore South started with ♠A972. You desperately want a diamond played through dummy's queen, so try the effect of the ♠8 (the highest spade you can afford) as a suit-preference signal. West ruffs and leads the ♦10, and try as he may, declarer cannot now come to ten tricks. The contract succeeds easily on any other defense.

Even more than bidding, defense is the aspect of the game that requires absolute partnership harmony. Looking just at your own cards and dummy will not enable you to solve many defensive problems. You must also be able to count partner's shape and high cards. We have seen how important it is for one defender to provide the other with information. If you can defend as if you can see all four hands at the point that critical decisions need to be made, your results will improve significantly.

Once you can see the winning defense, take control if you can. Just because you know the whole hand, do not assume partner also does. Perhaps he should know what is going on but has been taking a nap. If you can beat the contract without giving partner a decision to make (even if it should be obvious to him), then do so. Do not give him a chance to make a mistake. Here is an example of what we mean:

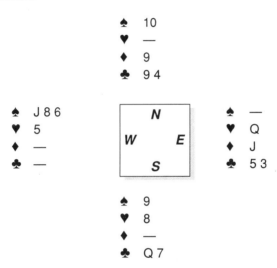

This is the ending in a notrump contract. As West, you have gained the lead with a club winner. You have three winning spades and a losing heart. You know your partner has a winning heart and a winning diamond. Many West players would cash their three spade tricks without thinking.

But at Trick 12, partner may do the wrong thing by keeping his diamond winner and throwing his heart. Perhaps partner's defense is only right if there are fourteen diamonds in the deck, but the error is totally yours — you gave him a losing option when it wasn't necessary. If you take only two spade winners and then play your heart, partner will take the last two tricks without having been put to the test.

When planning your defense, try to envisage potential problems from partner's point of view. What may be obvious to you may not be so to him. Make him do the right thing. This is such an important point that it is worth a second example:

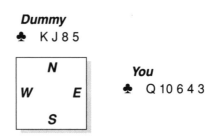

Dummy

♣ K J 8 5

You

♣ Q 10 6 4 3

This is a side suit in a trump contract. You get an early count and you realize that declarer has a singleton in this suit. Once declarer has drawn partner's trumps he will probably lead his singleton. You also know that all partner has to do to beat the contract is to jump up with his ace. How do you ensure that partner cannot get this wrong?

Let's say you have a chance to signal your length in the suit by discarding the ♣3. Declarer duly leads a club, partner ducks, declarer wins the king, and the contract makes. Yes, you can explain learnedly to partner that you gave him count and he should have worked out that declarer had a singleton. But do you think partner would have ducked his ace if instead you had discarded the ♣Q? Georgio Duboin, a rising young Italian star, once paid Pietro Forquet a great compliment when he said of him, 'He doesn't let you make a mistake.'

There are hands on which you appear to have a complete guess; nevertheless, playing with a thoughtful partner, you can defend on the basis that he would have made things obvious for you if he could. You might not consider that this final hand belongs in the category of 'signalling', but remember — it is not always what partner does that helps you, but sometimes what he does not do. How do you defend with these West cards?

Both Vul.
Lead: ♣5

    ♠ J 9 5
    ♥ A K
    ♦ Q J 9 7 5
    ♣ K J 9

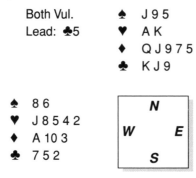

♠ 8 6
♥ J 8 5 4 2
♦ A 10 3
♣ 7 5 2

WEST	NORTH	EAST	SOUTH
pass	1♦	2♣	2♠
pass	2NT	pass	4♠
all pass			

Declarer plays the ♣9 from dummy, partner wins the ten and returns the ♦6, on which declarer plays low. Do you win or duck? If you win, do you play a second club through or try to give partner a diamond ruff?

Partner cannot have too much in the way of high cards, so he must surely have six clubs for his vulnerable two-level overcall. Let's say partner has a singleton diamond and you can give him a ruff — can you get a fourth trick from anywhere? Clearly declarer's red suits are solid. You have already decided there is no second club trick. Therefore, if you are to beat the contract, partner must have the ace of trumps. So do you take the first diamond and play partner for a singleton?

The answer is no, not if you are playing with a thoughtful partner. To understand why, consider how you would defend if partner cashed the ♠A before leading his diamond. You would now have no choice but to play him for a singleton. If partner had that hand he would have made the defense obvious for you. The only explanation for his failure to defend in this way is that he has two diamonds. You must therefore duck your ace. This is the full hand:

```
              ♠  J 9 5
              ♥  A K
              ♦  Q J 9 7 5
              ♣  K J 9

♠  8 6                          ♠  A 2
♥  J 8 5 4 2        N            ♥  9 7 3
♦  A 10 3      W        E        ♦  6 2
♣  7 5 2           S            ♣  A Q 10 6 4 3

              ♠  K Q 10 7 4 3
              ♥  Q 10 6
              ♦  K 8 4
              ♣  8
```

LESSONS FROM THIS CHAPTER

- The objective of signalling is to tell partner about your hand, *not* to tell him what to do.

- Signals are *not* instructions. It is up to you to decide how to defend, based on what partner tells you about his hand.

- Combine attitude, count and suit-preference signals depending on what information is needed.

- Do not bother to signal information that is useless to partner. Tell him what you think he needs or wants to know.

- If you can see the winning defense, take control. If you can avoid doing so, do not put partner in a situation where he can do the wrong thing.

- Do not just consider what partner *has* done. Think about what he has *not* done, too.

- When you have what appears to be a guess, consider how partner might have helped you solve the problem. If he has not made the defense clear, then assume he does not have a hand that would enable him to do so and defend accordingly.

CHAPTER 13

Counting Declarer's Shape

We have seen that you can greatly improve your chances as declarer by determining the shape of the unseen hands. The same applies when you are defending, and again, counting is the route to success.

As a defender, you have a head start on the counting process, since the auction must almost inevitably give you information about declarer's hand. Putting this together with the information that the lead and play to the first trick gives you can sometimes allow you to 'see' the entire hand from a very early stage of the proceedings. Without counting, you would have little chance of finding the winning play on our first deal:

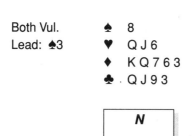

Both Vul.
Lead: ♠3

```
                ♠  8
                ♥  Q J 6
                ♦  K Q 7 6 3
                ♣  Q J 9 3
                              ♠  A J 7 5 2
              N               ♥  5
          W       E           ♦  8 4
              S               ♣  K 8 6 4 2
```

WEST	NORTH	EAST	SOUTH
			1♥
pass	2♦	pass	3♦
pass	4♥	all pass	

Partner leads the ♠3 (fourth-highest) to your ace. What now? South probably has five hearts (as he might have rebid a six-card suit) and four diamonds. Partner's lead marks South with three spades too, so the most likely shape for declarer is 3-5-4-1. That leaves partner with four trumps. Partner cannot have enough high cards to beat the contract on sheer power. The only chance is to make declarer ruff twice, and establish a trump trick for partner.

Obviously, the only suit in which you can force declarer is clubs. However, if you play a club to partner's presumed ace, your king will be ruffed on the second round of the suit. Dummy's remaining honor will then protect declarer from being forced a second time. All is not lost, though. Can you see what happens if you switch to the ♣K? Look at the full hand:

```
                ♠  8
                ♥  Q J 6
                ♦  K Q 7 6 3
                ♣  Q J 9 3

    ♠  Q 9 6 3                        ♠  A J 7 5 2
    ♥  K 8 7 2          N             ♥  5
    ♦  9 5          W       E         ♦  8 4
    ♣  A 7 5            S             ♣  K 8 6 4 2

                ♠  K 10 4
                ♥  A 10 9 4 3
                ♦  A J 10 2
                ♣  10
```

Your ♣K holds and declarer must ruff the club continuation. When partner wins his ♥K he will be able to lead the ♣A, forcing declarer for a second time and establishing his own long trump as the fourth defensive trick.

In this instance, you could estimate the length of two of declarer's suits from his bidding and a third from the opening lead, giving you an inferential count immediately. Always be alert to the limits the bidding places on declarer's distribution. This is particularly true if he has opened 1NT, when his shape is defined within very limited parameters. You can reasonably assume that it will be 4333, 4432 or 5332 (although some declarers will occasionally show up with a six-card minor or a 5422 shape).

These limits on declarer's distribution, plus the certainty of an entry in partner's hand from a count of the high card points, should lead you to the winning defense with the East cards on our next deal. If you are feeling energetic, take the East seat and cover the West and South hands.

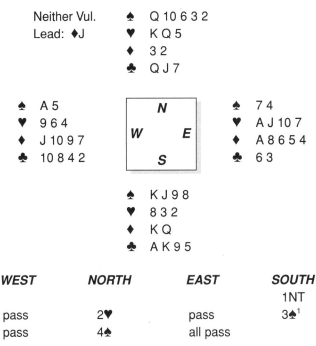

Neither Vul.	♠	Q 10 6 3 2
Lead: ♦J	♥	K Q 5
	♦	3 2
	♣	Q J 7

West:
♠ A 5
♥ 9 6 4
♦ J 10 9 7
♣ 10 8 4 2

East:
♠ 7 4
♥ A J 10 7
♦ A 8 6 5 4
♣ 6 3

South:
♠ K J 9 8
♥ 8 3 2
♦ K Q
♣ A K 9 5

WEST	NORTH	EAST	SOUTH
			1NT
pass	2♥	pass	3♠[1]
pass	4♠	all pass	

1. Good four-card spade fit

You overtake the ♦J at trick one and declarer follows with the queen. How do you continue? It looks like South has four spades and the ♦KQ doubleton. Because of his opening 1NT, you can reasonably expect him to be 3-4 or 4-3 in the other two suits. A count of the missing high cards confirms that partner has an entry. Declarer has 15-17 points, leaving partner 4-6 points. Your two aces

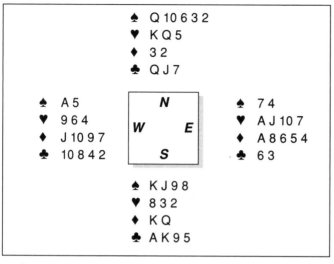

♠ Q 10 6 3 2
♥ K Q 5
♦ 3 2
♣ Q J 7

♠ A 5
♥ 9 6 4
♦ J 10 9 7
♣ 10 8 4 2

N W E S

♠ 7 4
♥ A J 10 7
♦ A 8 6 5 4
♣ 6 3

♠ K J 9 8
♥ 8 3 2
♦ K Q
♣ A K 9 5

*diagram
repeated
for convenience*

and partner's black-suit ace or king will give you three defensive tricks, but you must establish your fourth trick before partner's entry is removed. Having reached this conclusion, you should see that the ♥J is clearly the correct return. When West wins his ♠A, he will return a heart through dummy's remaining honor and the ♥10 will be your fourth trick.

Preemptive bids give away considerable information, but against high-level contracts it is often critical that you take your winners before they disappear. The next deal is typical, and illustrates why accurate signalling is vital.

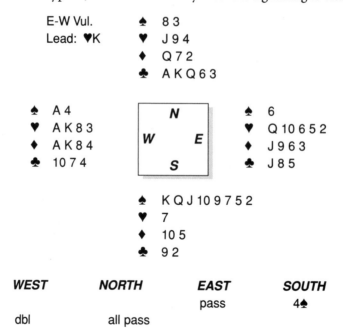

E-W Vul.
Lead: ♥K

♠ 8 3
♥ J 9 4
♦ Q 7 2
♣ A K Q 6 3

♠ A 4
♥ A K 8 3
♦ A K 8 4
♣ 10 7 4

N W E S

♠ 6
♥ Q 10 6 5 2
♦ J 9 6 3
♣ J 8 5

♠ K Q J 10 9 7 5 2
♥ 7
♦ 10 5
♣ 9 2

WEST	NORTH	EAST	SOUTH
		pass	4♠
dbl	all pass		

It probably doesn't matter which ace-king you lead and this time you opt for hearts. You lead the king (requesting count) and partner's ♥2 indicates an odd number of hearts. When you try the ♦K, the news is better: partner follows with the ♦9. Since declarer must have at least one more diamond, you know you can cash the ♦A to beat the contract. If you were not playing count signals, you would defeat this contract only one time in two as you would have to guess which red winner to try to cash at Trick 3.

Now let's change the hands slightly:

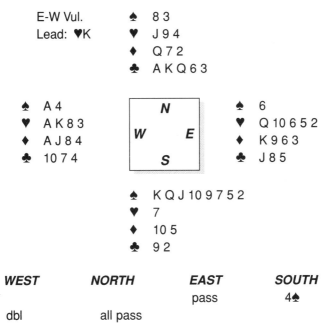

E-W Vul.
Lead: ♥K

	♠ 8 3
	♥ J 9 4
	♦ Q 7 2
	♣ A K Q 6 3

♠ A 4   ♠ 6
♥ A K 8 3 ♥ Q 10 6 5 2
♦ A J 8 4 ♦ K 9 6 3
♣ 10 7 4   ♣ J 8 5

♠ K Q J 10 9 7 5 2
♥ 7
♦ 10 5
♣ 9 2

WEST	NORTH	EAST	SOUTH
		pass	4♠
dbl	all pass		

The play to Trick 1 is the same — partner plays the ♥2 on your ♥K. Now you have a choice — does partner have the ♦K or should you try to cash another heart trick? Note that on the first layout you led the king from ace-king because you wanted partner to give count. Count signals after high-level pre-empts are essential but sometimes you need to know if partner likes a suit. It is useful to use the lead of the ace and king to ask for different information.

On this new layout, you try the ♦A at Trick 2. Partner again plays the ♦9, but this time it is an attitude signal rather than a count card. Partner is not telling you to play a second diamond without thinking, but is simply letting you know that he has the king. If, for example, you had only ♥AKx, then you would know a second round of hearts was standing up and you would cash the ♥A before playing a second round of diamonds.

Let's change the hand again:

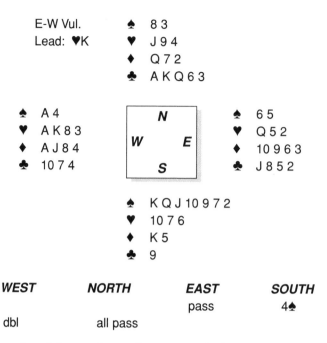

		E-W Vul.	♠ 8 3		
		Lead: ♥K	♥ J 9 4		
			♦ Q 7 2		
			♣ A K Q 6 3		

♠ A 4   ♠ 6 5
♥ A K 8 3   ♥ Q 5 2
♦ A J 8 4   ♦ 10 9 6 3
♣ 10 7 4   ♣ J 8 5 2

♠ K Q J 10 9 7 2
♥ 10 7 6
♦ K 5
♣ 9

WEST	NORTH	EAST	SOUTH
		pass	4♠
dbl	all pass		

Your hand and dummy's are the same as before, and once again, partner plays the ♥2 under your ♥K to show an odd number of hearts at Trick 1. This time, though, when you continue with the ♦A, partner follows with the ♦3, denying the king. Now your only chance is that partner started with only three hearts and not five, so you play the ♥A. When everyone follows, you play a third heart. Since partner has the queen, the contract goes two down.

In all three situations, it was a combination of count and attitude signals that enabled you to find the optimum defense. Sometimes accurate signalling alone is not enough and you will have to work harder when a preemptor becomes declarer. The range for a three-level (or higher) opening can be very wide, but a weak two usually falls within well-defined parameters, particularly when the premptor is vulnerable. This will often enable you to build an accurate picture of declarer's hand almost immediately. Try to do this as you look at the next single-dummy problem.

(See the hand at top of the next page.)

Your ♣K holds Trick 1 as partner follows with the ♣2, and the ♣Q wins the next trick. What do you play now, and why?

It looks safe to play a third club, but before doing so try to build a picture of the two unseen hands. South has six spades and two clubs. Since you can reasonably expect that declarer has not opened a vulnerable weak two with a suit headed by the ten, you can count him for at least eight tricks — six trumps

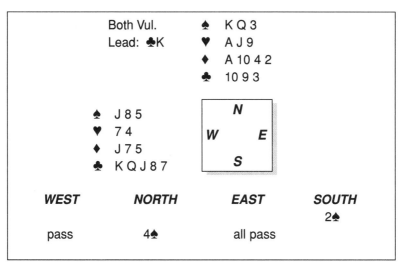

Both Vul.	♠ K Q 3
Lead: ♣K	♥ A J 9
	♦ A 10 4 2
	♣ 10 9 3

	♠ J 8 5		
	♥ 7 4		N
	♦ J 7 5	W E
	♣ K Q J 8 7		S

WEST	NORTH	EAST	SOUTH
			2♠
pass	4♠	all pass	

and dummy's two aces. If declarer has no other high cards, or just the ♥Q and two or three small diamonds, any continuation will beat the contract.

The danger occurs when declarer has ♦Qxx (with either ♥Qx or two small hearts). On that layout, if you play another club, declarer will draw trumps and lead towards the ♦Q. In time, his heart loser will disappear on the fourth round of diamonds. The same thing will happen if you switch to a diamond. Playing a heart now can hardly ever cost, and may be vital. This is the full hand:

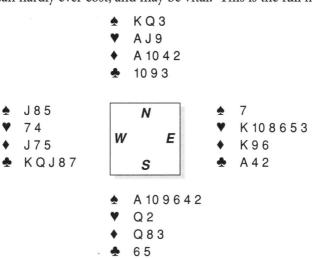

	♠ K Q 3	
	♥ A J 9	
	♦ A 10 4 2	
	♣ 10 9 3	

♠ J 8 5		♠ 7
♥ 7 4	N	♥ K 10 8 6 5 3
♦ J 7 5	W E	♦ K 9 6
♣ K Q J 8 7	S	♣ A 4 2

	♠ A 10 9 6 4 2	
	♥ Q 2	
	♦ Q 8 3	
	♣ 6 5	

When defending against a sacrifice, accurate signalling is usually required to extract the maximum penalty. When the location of most of the high cards is known from the bidding, the defense is normally based on a combination of count and suit-preference signals. Our next hand occurred in a team-of-four match at a recent Australian National Championships. The North-South pair found a profitable save but the defense was at its best:

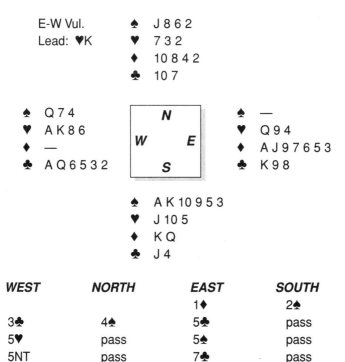

E-W Vul.
Lead: ♥K

```
                  ♠ J 8 6 2
                  ♥ 7 3 2
                  ♦ 10 8 4 2
                  ♣ 10 7

♠ Q 7 4                          ♠ —
♥ A K 8 6          N             ♥ Q 9 4
♦ —            W       E         ♦ A J 9 7 6 5 3
♣ A Q 6 5 3 2      S             ♣ K 9 8

                  ♠ A K 10 9 5 3
                  ♥ J 10 5
                  ♦ K Q
                  ♣ J 4
```

WEST	NORTH	EAST	SOUTH
		1♦	2♠
3♣	4♠	5♣	pass
5♥	pass	5♠	pass
5NT	pass	7♣	pass
pass	7♠	dbl	all pass

West led the ♥K and East played the ♥4 (showing an odd number) at Trick 1. The location of the ♣K was known from East's acceptance of the 5NT grand slam try, so when West cashed the ♣A at trick two East gave count with the ♣8. Although declarer played the ♣J, West knew the ♣8 was East's lowest club since he would have played second highest (the nine) from ♣K984.

West continued with the ♣2 (a clear suit-preference signal for a diamond) to East's king. East obediently cashed the ♦A and played the ♦J (another suit-preference signal, showing the ♥Q) for West to ruff. Knowing (from East's count signal at trick one) that hearts were 4-3-3-3 around the table, West cashed the king and led a third round to East's queen. East-West had taken the first seven tricks and declarer was down to just AK10xxx of trumps, but the defense had not finished. A third round of diamonds promoted the ♠Q for the defenders' eighth trick. That was +2000. Although this was less than the +2140 E/W would have made in 7♣, their teammates defended 6♣ for -1390. The reward for accurate defense was therefore 12 IMPs.

When defending against game and partscore contracts you may have numerous decisions to make, some of which will not be fatal if you get them wrong. Against a slam, however, you usually only get one chance:

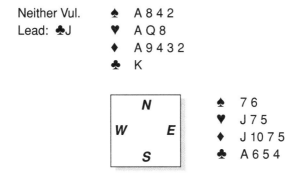

Neither Vul.	♠ A 8 4 2
Lead: ♣J	♥ A Q 8
	♦ A 9 4 3 2
	♣ K

	♠ 7 6
	♥ J 7 5
	♦ J 10 7 5
	♣ A 6 5 4

WEST	NORTH	EAST	SOUTH
			1NT[1]
pass	2♣	pass	2♥
pass	6NT	all pass	

1. 15-17 HCP

Plan the defense.

Dummy has seventeen points and you have six. Add declarer's minimum of fifteen and that leaves at most two points for partner, one of which you saw on his opening lead. This means that declarer has at least the ♠KQ, ♥Kxxx, the ♦KQ and the ♣Q. You can see hearts are breaking 3-3, so you can count eleven tricks — four hearts, three diamonds, three spades and a club. If declarer has the ♠J, or any four spades, he has twelve top tricks, so assume he doesn't. If you are to have any chance, declarer's hand must be something like:

    ♠ K Q x
    ♥ K x x x
    ♦ K Q ?   (?=either/or)
    ♣ Q x x ?

Before doing anything, you should mentally play through the complete hand. Let's say you take dummy's ♣K with the ♣A and return a club. South will cash his seven red-suit winners, and with four cards left partner will have to keep ♠Jxxx and a club stopper. Oops! That's too many cards for a four-card ending... here is the full hand:

```
              ♠ A 8 4 2
              ♥ A Q 8
              ♦ A 9 4 3 2
              ♣ K

♠ J 9 5 3        ┌─────────┐        ♠ 7 6
♥ 4 3 2          │    N    │        ♥ J 7 5
♦ 8 6            │ W     E │        ♦ J 10 7 5
♣ J 10 9 3       │    S    │        ♣ A 6 5 4
                 └─────────┘
              ♠ K Q 10
              ♥ K 10 9 6
              ♦ K Q
              ♣ Q 8 7 2
```

It is often possible to see that you are going to be squeezed. Foreseeing the same thing happening to partner requires much greater vision and awareness. On this hand, the solution is relatively simple provided you stop to count *before* you let your only chance to beat the contract pass you by. If you allow the ♣K to hold at trick one, declarer can never cash enough winners to put partner under pressure and the contract will just drift quietly down.

Many players would have let this slam make before they even thought about the defense. As we have stressed time and again, you should count your tricks as declarer before you play any card to Trick 1. The same is true on defense. As a defender you should count your potential tricks as well as declarer's tricks. Information from the bidding will usually allow you to count most of the high-card points, and frequently you will be able to judge the likely distribution of the closed hands too. Mentally playing through the hand before you commit yourself to a particular line of defense will reap enormous rewards. (You might also have found the winning defense on this hand by applying another sound defensive principle: if you cannot see a way to defeat the contract by winning a trick, try the effect of ducking.)

LESSONS FROM THIS CHAPTER

- When you have long trumps, it is often obvious to defend in a manner that forces declarer to ruff. When you have short trumps, try to view the hand from partner's perspective and work to establish trump control for him by forcing declarer.

- When declarer has made an opening notrump bid, you can immediately place him with one of a small number of possible shapes. You can defend on the assumption that he will not have a singleton.

- When defending against preempts, be prepared to cash your tricks quickly. Use count and attitude signals to make sure you cash your tricks in the right order.

- Work out the various hands declarer may have. If your defense only makes a difference if he has one of these hands, assume he has that hand and defend accordingly.

- When defending against high-level sacrifices, use count and suit-preference signals to take the maximum penalty.

- Look at the hand from both declarer's and partner's viewpoint. Try to foresee potential problems that partner may have, and defend in a way that avoids putting him under pressure.

CHAPTER 14

Counting Declarer's Points

If you become declarer after an uncontested auction, you will have little or no information about the location of the missing high cards. Defenders are never quite so handicapped since declarer must, by definition, have made a positive bid. In many cases, the strength and shape of declarer's hand will be known within fairly limited parameters. By inference therefore, you will also know a great deal about your partner's hand.

For example, you may know that partner has 3-4 points. You will usually be able to work out that he has one of two or three specific cards. Using this information, you should imagine the whole hand and see how the play is likely to go if partner has each of the possible holdings. If only one of the scenarios allows you to beat the contract, assume that is the one that exists and defend accordingly.

During the period when they were training to take on the legendary Italian Blue Team, the Dallas Aces established a number of maxims, both for partnerships and for individuals. One of these was to avoid 'no play' defenses. Our first hand illustrates this concept:

```
Both Vul.          ♠  A Q J 5
Lead: ♣K           ♥  9 4
                   ♦  A K 5
                   ♣  J 10 9 4

        ♠  8 7 3            N
        ♥  K J 10 5
        ♦  8 4         W         E
        ♣  A K 6 3
                            S
```

WEST	NORTH	EAST	SOUTH
			1♥
pass	1♠	pass	1NT
pass	3NT	all pass	

North-South play five-card majors and a strong notrump, so South's rebid shows 12-14 points. You lead the ♣K and see the ♣5 from partner and the ♣8 from declarer. What now?

You can see twenty-six points between your hand and dummy, and declarer has at least twelve of the other fourteen, leaving partner with, at most, one of the missing queens. Let's construct each of the possible hands and count declarer's tricks. If partner has the ♦Q, declarer will be able to force out your second top club and he will eventually make four spade tricks, two clubs, two diamonds and the ♥A. The ♣Q with partner will not help either. You can make three clubs and a heart but declarer will come to four spades, three diamonds, a heart and a club. Conclusion — if partner's two points are a minor-suit queen, the contract is destined to make.

Although it means leading into the five-card suit bid by declarer, your only hope is to switch to a small heart at Trick 2. If declarer has the ♥Q then of course he will make his contract, probably with overtricks, but in that case you were never going plus. However, if partner has ♥Qx you will defeat the contract (unless declarer has four diamond tricks). Any play at trick two other than the ♥5 is just giving up — a 'no play' defense. You are playing for the full hand to be something like:

```
          ♠ A Q J 5
          ♥ 9 4
          ♦ A K 5
          ♣ J 10 9 4

♠ 8 7 3          N          ♠ 10 6 4 2
♥ K J 10 5                  ♥ Q 7
♦ 8 4      W         E      ♦ 10 9 6 3 2
♣ A K 6 3        S          ♣ 5 2

          ♠ K 9
          ♥ A 8 6 3 2
          ♦ Q J 7
          ♣ Q 8 7
```

Partner cannot have many high cards on our next exhibit either. As before, counting points is easy as declarer has a limited hand — he has opened with a notrump bid. Once again, you must work out a possible hand for partner that will allow you to defeat the contract, and then defend on the assumption that he has that hand.

```
E-W Vul.    ♠ 8 6 5 2
Lead: ♦K    ♥ A Q 9 5
            ♦ 5 3 2
            ♣ Q 7

                                ♠ J 10 9 3
            N                   ♥ J 8 3
      W           E             ♦ A 8 7 6
            S                   ♣ 10 5
```

WEST	NORTH	EAST	SOUTH
		pass	2NT
pass	3♣	pass	3♥
pass	4♥	all pass	

South's 2NT opening shows 20-22 points. Partner leads the ♦K, and continues with the ♦Q and the ♦10, declarer following to the first two diamonds. How do you plan to defeat this contract?

You can see fourteen points between dummy and your own hand. Thus, the unseen hands have twenty-six points between them and partner has already

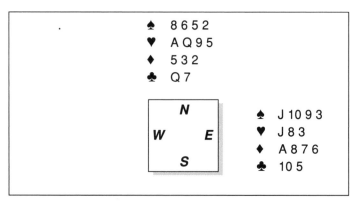

shown up with five in diamonds. That leaves twenty-one points and declarer must have them all (except, perhaps, the useless ♣J).

You know declarer will follow to all three diamonds (as partner didn't lead the jack at Trick 3) but you still need to find a fourth defensive trick. Since declarer must have ♣AK and ♠AKQ, the only possible source of that fourth trick is the trump suit. There is only one card that partner can have which is of any use — ♥10. You should win the ♦A and play a fourth round of diamonds, giving declarer a useless ruff and discard. This will allow partner to ruff with the ♥10 if he has it, forcing out one of dummy's honors. Your ♥J83 will then be promoted into the setting trick.

Unless the hand is something like that shown below, you can never beat the contract:

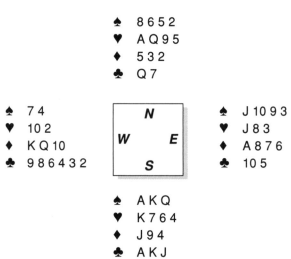

The theme is similar on the next hand in that West must count declarer's points and shape. This time, he must also draw an inference from his partner's play. If you feel like a mental workout, take over from West and cover the East and South hands.

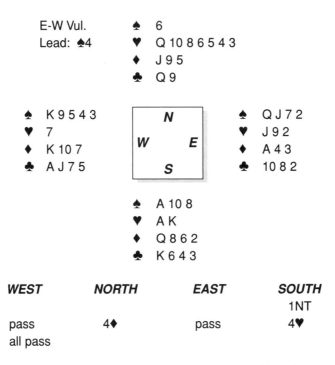

E-W Vul.
Lead: ♠4

♠ 6
♥ Q 10 8 6 5 4 3
♦ J 9 5
♣ Q 9

♠ K 9 5 4 3
♥ 7
♦ K 10 7
♣ A J 7 5

♠ Q J 7 2
♥ J 9 2
♦ A 4 3
♣ 10 8 2

♠ A 10 8
♥ A K
♦ Q 8 6 2
♣ K 6 4 3

WEST	NORTH	EAST	SOUTH
			1NT
pass	4♦	pass	4♥
all pass			

South's 1NT opening shows 15-17 points, and North's 4♦ is a Texas Transfer to hearts. Partner's ♠J loses to the ♠A at trick one. Declarer cashes the ♥AK and ruffs a spade in dummy. He then draws East's outstanding trump with the ♥Q, and leads the ♣Q. How do you plan to defend?

Essentially, the contract depends upon declarer guessing which defender has the ♦10. However, despite his sixteen points, entries to the South hand are a problem, and to protect your ♦10 you must duck dummy's ♣Q. South has shown up with the ♠A and the ♥AK. If your partner had the ♣K he would have covered the queen, so South has that card, bringing his known points to fourteen. Declarer cannot have the ♦A as that would give him an 18-count, but he must have the ♦Q to make up his 15-17 points. The defense has three certain tricks and you can see the danger posed by dummy's ♦9 if declarer is allowed an entry to hand with the ♣K.

As an aside, it is worth looking at this hand from declarer's perspective. Against expert defenders, if West takes the ♣A on the first round, whom should you play to hold the ♦10? You should finesse against East on the assumption that West would duck the club if he had the ♦10. By allowing you to reach your hand, West is giving you a losing option. As we have noted elsewhere, you should always be wary of good defenders bearing gifts...

Counting declarer's hand to see if it is possible for partner to have a vital card is essential when you have most of your side's assets. The danger of an endplay or squeeze should be uppermost in your mind on these occasions. If you can construct a hand for declarer that is consistent with the bidding which allows you to defeat the contract, play for that layout to exist.

Desperate times call for desperate measures, and you should occasionally be prepared to break even the oldest maxims in bridge. Cover the East and South cards and see if you can spot the winning defense from the West seat.

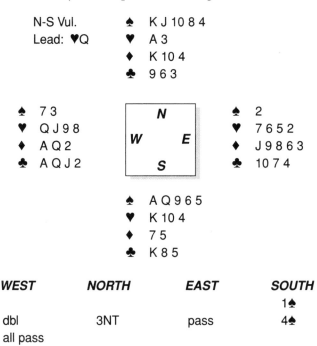

N-S Vul.	♠	K J 10 8 4
Lead: ♥Q	♥	A 3
	♦	K 10 4
	♣	9 6 3

West:
♠ 7 3
♥ Q J 9 8
♦ A Q 2
♣ A Q J 2

East:
♠ 2
♥ 7 6 5 2
♦ J 9 8 6 3
♣ 10 7 4

South:
♠ A Q 9 6 5
♥ K 10 4
♦ 7 5
♣ K 8 5

WEST	NORTH	EAST	SOUTH
			1♠
dbl	3NT	pass	4♠
all pass			

North's 3NT shows a good raise to at least 4♠ and South's sign-off suggests a minimum opening bid. Dummy's ♥A takes your ♥Q at Trick 1 and trumps are drawn in two rounds, partner following once and then discarding the ♦3 (showing an odd number). Declarer now leads a diamond towards dummy. How do you plan to beat this contract?

Let's say you follow with your small diamond... declarer wins the ♦K, plays the ♥K, ruffs a heart, and exits with a diamond to your queen. You try to get off lead with the ♦A, but declarer discards a club from his hand. You must now give him a ruff and discard or lead a club around to his king. Either way, you make just three tricks.

Perhaps you should win the ♦A and exit with the queen. Now declarer cannot endplay you in diamonds but... he wins the ♦K, ruffs dummy's third diamond, and now plays the king and ten of hearts. When you cover with the jack, declarer discards a club from dummy, and once again you are endplayed to concede the tenth trick.

To defeat this hand, both defenders must be alert. Partner's ♦3 told you that declarer has a doubleton diamond. There are thirteen points missing, and declarer does not have an opening bid if he is missing any honor other than the ♦J, so that is the card you must play for East to hold.

See what happens if you play the queen on the first diamond. The king wins, but when declarer attempts to endplay you with a second diamond, your partner is able to win the trick. The defense is not quite home yet, though. East must realize that this is the only time he will be on lead. If he plays a club to your jack, you can exit safely with the ♦A, but when declarer runs his trumps, you will be strip-squeezed and later endplayed with the ♣A to lead into the ♥K10. East must table the ♣10 when he has the lead. Declarer is then powerless to stop the defense scoring three club tricks and one diamond.

Our final hand occurred in the 1998 Australian Team Trials. Sitting West, Ben Thompson demonstrated, in spectacular fashion, what can be done when a defender knows the location of all the high cards:

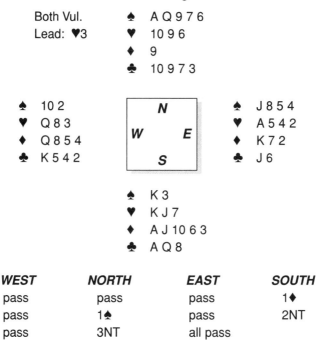

Both Vul.	♠ A Q 9 7 6
Lead: ♥3	♥ 10 9 6
	♦ 9
	♣ 10 9 7 3

WEST	NORTH	EAST	SOUTH
pass	pass	pass	1♦
pass	1♠	pass	2NT
pass	3NT	all pass	

East took the first trick with the ♥A and returned the suit to declarer's jack and the queen. After winning the third round of hearts with the king, declarer

```
            ♠ A Q 9 7 6
            ♥ 10 9 6
            ♦ 9
            ♣ 10 9 7 3

♠ 10 2          N          ♠ J 8 5 4
♥ Q 8 3                    ♥ A 5 4 2
♦ Q 8 5 4   W       E      ♦ K 7 2
♣ K 5 4 2         S        ♣ J 6

            ♠ K 3
            ♥ K J 7
            ♦ A J 10 6 3
            ♣ A Q 8
```

played off three top spades, discarding the ♦3 while Thompson (West) shed a club. Now came a club to the queen — and Thompson ducked, a key move that limited declarer to two club tricks.

Now the ♣A from declarer followed by the ♣8 put West on play. Thompson exited with a diamond to the king and ace. Declarer tried the ♦J now, but Thompson hadn't come this far to fall at the last hurdle. He ducked this trick, too, and now held ♦Q8 over declarer's ♦106. One down!

The vital play was Thompson's duck of the ♣Q. Declarer had shown up with the ♥KJ, the ♠K and the ♣Q — nine points. If he did not have the ♣A, he would always go down, and if he did have the ♣A, then he could not have the ♦AK as well. That would give him twenty points when his 2NT rebid showed only eighteen to nineteen.

LESSONS FROM THIS CHAPTER

- Count the points in your hand and dummy and add those that declarer has shown in the bidding. You will then have a narrow range of points for partner's hand.

- Avoid 'no play' defenses. Do not play partner for a specific card if you cannot defeat the contract, even when he has that card.

- If you need partner to have a specific card to beat the contract, defend on the assumption that he has it.

- When you have most of your side's high cards, be wary of squeezes or endplays. Look for ways to put partner on lead.

CHAPTER 15

Counting Declarer's Tricks

In the last two chapters, we have tried to build a picture of declarer's hand by counting his shape and his high card points. Many defenders get that far, and then fail to take the next vital step — counting declarer's tricks.

Counting tricks is as critical for defenders as it is for declarer. It is the final piece of information that you need to plan your defensive strategy. Is declarer scrambling in a tight contract? Then play passively, and make sure you don't surrender tricks unnecessarily. Can you count enough sure tricks that he's going to cash out as soon as you let him in? Then you need to find tricks fast, and anything that has a chance of working is worth a try.

We begin with a straightforward example:

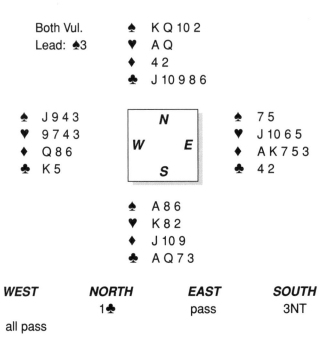

Both Vul.
Lead: ♠3

	♠ K Q 10 2	
	♥ A Q	
	♦ 4 2	
	♣ J 10 9 8 6	

♠ J 9 4 3	N	♠ 7 5
♥ 9 7 4 3	W E	♥ J 10 6 5
♦ Q 8 6		♦ A K 7 5 3
♣ K 5	S	♣ 4 2

	♠ A 8 6	
	♥ K 8 2	
	♦ J 10 9	
	♣ A Q 7 3	

WEST	NORTH	EAST	SOUTH
	1♣	pass	3NT
all pass			

Having little information to go on, you lead your fourth highest spade. Declarer wins with dummy's king and runs the ♣J to your king. What now?

A lazy defender might switch to a heart, perhaps with some vague hope of finding his partner with the king. A count of declarer's tricks makes it clear that such a switch is unlikely to bear fruit (unless declarer's 3NT bid was a wild gamble, and he holds ♣Qxxx and either ♥Jx or ♥xxx). Let's imagine for a moment that East has the ♥K instead of the ♦K. If you switch to a heart, declarer will probably finesse and lose the trick to partner's king, but even if he misguesses on the diamond return, he will still make 3NT. The defense make the ♦Q, the ♣K, the ♦A and the ♥K which only adds up to four tricks. Not enough!

If you stop to count declarer's tricks when you take the ♣K, you will see that he can make four spades (with the aid of the marked finesse against your jack), four clubs (even if partner has the queen) plus dummy's ♥A. That adds up to nine. This simple count makes it clear that you must take four tricks right now. Obviously, the only hope is diamonds, and on the actual hand partner will be delighted with your switch.

Our next hand occurred in the final of the 1970 Australian National IMP Pairs. Try it as a problem:

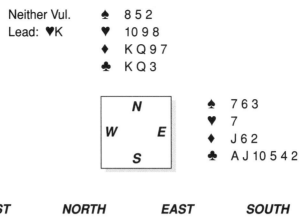

Neither Vul. ♠ 8 5 2
Lead: ♥K   ♥ 10 9 8
           ♦ K Q 9 7
           ♣ K Q 3

                   ♠ 7 6 3
                   ♥ 7
                   ♦ J 6 2
                   ♣ A J 10 5 4 2

WEST	NORTH	EAST	SOUTH
			1♠
2♥	3♥	pass	4♠
all pass			

North's 3♥ bid shows a sound spade raise. Partner leads the ♥K, followed by the ♥A and the ♥Q. What do you discard on the second and third hearts?

In real life, only three declarers failed in 4♠, but one of those was the great Tim Seres. He was unlucky enough to be at the table where Dr. Reg Busch, of Queensland, was East. This was the full hand:

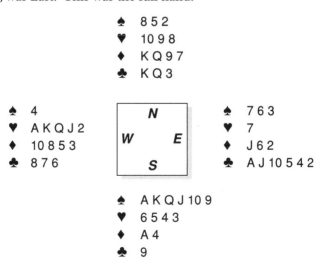

         ♠ 8 5 2
         ♥ 10 9 8
         ♦ K Q 9 7
         ♣ K Q 3

♠ 4   ♠ 7 6 3
♥ A K Q J 2   ♥ 7
♦ 10 8 5 3   ♦ J 6 2
♣ 8 7 6   ♣ A J 10 5 4 2

         ♠ A K Q J 10 9
         ♥ 6 5 4 3
         ♦ A 4
         ♣ 9

In Chapter 12, we introduced the idea that you should take control whenever you can see the winning defense. This is a classic illustration of this point. At most tables, East used his two discards to encourage a club switch. Is that what you did?

Move around to the West seat momentarily. It looks as though partner has the ♣A, but declarer could easily have a void. Doesn't it look tempting to play a fourth heart so that partner can overruff dummy? As you can see, this line of defense is not a success. It is easy to say that East signalled for a club and so West should switch to one; however, the blame for this disaster lies wholly with East, because he gave his partner a chance to do the wrong thing.

As East, you know you *cannot* overruff dummy. The only missing high cards are the ♦A and the trump honors, and declarer must have them all for his bidding. (Partner might have the ♠Q or the ♠J, but if he does it will surely be a singleton.) By counting declarer's tricks, you can see that if the ♣A is not a trick then the contract is unlikely to be beatable. So you should do what Busch did — discard a club on the second heart winner and one of your otherwise useless trumps on the third one. Having gained the lead by ruffing the ♥Q, you cash the ♣A to defeat the contract.

Acquiring the habit of counting declarer's tricks can also enable you to produce the occasional spectacular defense. Let's follow West's thought processes on the next hand:

```
          Both Vul.        ♠  A K 10 9
          Lead: ♥10        ♥  A Q 2
                           ♦  6 5 3
                           ♣  A 8 4

      ♠  6 3            ┌─────────┐        ♠  5 4 2
      ♥  10 9 7 6       │    N    │        ♥  K J 8 5 4
      ♦  J 8 7 2      W │         │ E      ♦  Q
      ♣  K 10 3         │    S    │        ♣  Q 9 7 6
                        └─────────┘

                           ♠  Q J 8 7
                           ♥  3
                           ♦  A K 10 9 4
                           ♣  J 5 2
```

WEST	NORTH	EAST	SOUTH
	1NT	pass	3♣[1]
pass	3♦	pass	3♠[2]
pass	4♣	pass	4♦
pass	4♥	pass	4♠
pass	6♠	all pass	

1. Transfer to diamonds
2. Second suit

Declarer wins the first trick with the ♥A and ruffs a heart. A trump to dummy's ten is followed by a second heart ruff. The ace and king of spades draw the outstanding trumps, and a diamond goes to the queen and king. As West, what do you do when declarer now plays the ♦10 in this position?

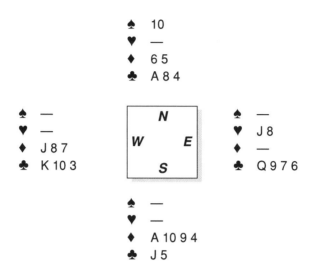

```
                        ♠  10
                        ♥  —
                        ♦  6 5
                        ♣  A 8 4

      ♠  —                N              ♠  —
      ♥  —                               ♥  J 8
      ♦  J 8 7      W           E        ♦  —
      ♣  K 10 3              S           ♣  Q 9 7 6

                        ♠  —
                        ♥  —
                        ♦  A 10 9 4
                        ♣  J 5
```

Many players would take the ♦J automatically — but if you stop to count declarer's tricks, it becomes apparent that the the ♦J will be your last trick. Declarer will make all the rest via three diamonds, the ♣A and dummy's trump. Refusing to take your jack leaves declarer with no entry and restricts him to three diamond tricks as opposed to four. You must, therefore, allow the ♦10 to hold.

Declarer plays a club to the ace and cashes his trump, discarding a diamond from hand. At the table, you would not know who had which club honor, but it is clear that if you keep the ♣K and ♦Jx then you will be endplayed to lead into declarer's diamond tenace at trick twelve. Concluding that if declarer's remaining club is the queen there is nothing you can do, you must assume your partner has the ♣Q and jettison the king. The contract is now doomed, despite a valiant effort by declarer.

West's defense may appear to be brilliant, but stopping to count declarer's tricks makes each step logical. Having said that, we all know plenty of defenders who would have slipped.

Now take the West cards and try your hand at this problem:

Neither Vul.   ♠ Q 7 5 3
Lead: ♥10   ♥ A Q
                 ♦ A 5
                 ♣ Q J 10 9 2

♠ K 9 2   N
♥ 10 9 8 6 2
♦ 9 6 4   W   E
♣ A 7
                            S

WEST	NORTH	EAST	SOUTH
			1NT
pass	2♣	pass	2♦
pass	3NT	all pass	

North-South reach 3NT after a 12-14 notrump opening and Stayman. Your heart lead is won by dummy's queen as partner follows with the ♥4 and declarer with the three. You allow the ♣Q to hold, and take the second round of the suit as partner plays the ♣8 and ♣5. What now?

By this point in the chapter, you should be acquiring the habit of stopping to count declarer's tricks. What is the heart position? Could declarer have had a doubleton king? Perhaps — but then partner would have started with ♥J764, from which he would have played high-low to show an even number. (You should not be fooled if declarer plays the ♥6 at trick one, as from ♥J743 partner would have given count with the ♥7 and not the ♥4.) Thus, declarer has three heart tricks, four club tricks and dummy's ♦A. That's eight. If he also has the ♠A, then the contract is untouchable, so mentally place that card in partner's hand. If declarer has the ♠J, then you still cannot take four tricks in the suit, so partner needs that too.

Clearly, you must lead a spade, but which one? The king cannot be right — even if partner has ♠AJ10x you will only get three tricks. What about the small spade? That will work if partner has the ten, but if declarer has that card dummy's queen will block the suit — small to the jack, back to your king, and now declarer plays low when you lead the ♠9, leaving partner with a spade winner but no entry. This is the full hand:

```
              ♠ Q 7 5 3
              ♥ A Q
              ♦ A 5
              ♣ Q J 10 9 2

♠ K 9 2                               ♠ A J 8 4
♥ 10 9 8 6 2     N                    ♥ J 7 4
♦ 9 6 4        W     E                ♦ 10 8 7 2
♣ A 7              S                  ♣ 8 5

              ♠ 10 6
              ♥ K 5 3
              ♦ K Q J 3
              ♣ K 6 4 3
```

As the cards lie, there is only one card you can lead to beat the contract. Did you find the switch to the ♠9? Does this look like an 'expert play' to you? Perhaps, but it is one that can be found by counting declarer's tricks and working out the minimum partner needs to beat the contract. You may think that partner will not be able to appreciate what you are doing, but remember that he is also counting declarer's tricks and points. He will know there is little hope for your side unless you hold the ♠K.

LESSONS FROM THIS CHAPTER

- Count declarer's high-card points and distribution, and then use that information to count his tricks.

- If you can see the winning defense, take control. Do not give partner a chance to go wrong.

- If a count of declarer's tricks reveals that partner needs a specific card (or cards) to beat the contract, then defend on the assumption that he has the required holding.

- Before you decide to play partner for a specific card, make sure that your defense will beat the contract if he has it.

CHAPTER 16

Concealing Your Distribution

Throughout this book we have seen how a competent declarer frequently finds the winning line of play by counting the defenders' shapes and high card points. Top-level defenders make this task more difficult for declarer.

In the previous four chapters, we concentrated on counting in terms of how it improves your own defensive accuracy. In the rest of the book, we are going to talk about various ways in which defenders can try to camouflage their holdings from an observant declarer. We begin with a look at ways in which you can prevent declarer from determining the shape of your hand.

It is often easy for a defender to play (or discard) a particular card because 'it seems obvious.' We have seen numerous examples of bids that provided declarer with the information he needed to make a contract. The same is also true of cards that are played. There are many hands on which declarer cannot get an accurate count of the distribution without help from the defenders.

Our first deal comes from a team-of-four match. Declarer must solve a two-way guess for a queen to bring home a grand slam. There are seven hearts missing and the queen is with the four-card holding, so you would expect a competent declarer to succeed, and he will — unless the defenders are extremely careful.

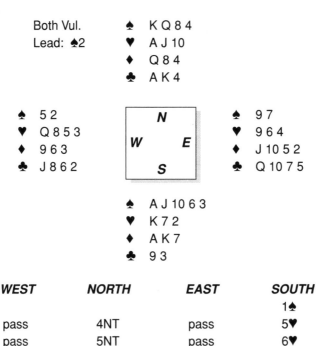

```
          Both Vul.        ♠  K Q 8 4
          Lead: ♠2         ♥  A J 10
                           ♦  Q 8 4
                           ♣  A K 4

     ♠  5 2                          ♠  9 7
     ♥  Q 8 5 3        N              ♥  9 6 4
     ♦  9 6 3     W         E         ♦  J 10 5 2
     ♣  J 8 6 2         S            ♣  Q 10 7 5

                           ♠  A J 10 6 3
                           ♥  K 7 2
                           ♦  A K 7
                           ♣  9 3
```

WEST	NORTH	EAST	SOUTH
			1♠
pass	4NT	pass	5♥
pass	5NT	pass	6♥
pass	7♠	all pass	

Declarer wins the trump lead and draws a second round. Hoping to get a count of the defensive hands, he plays off three rounds of diamonds (to which both defenders follow) and then two more rounds of trumps. West discards two clubs while East parts with the thirteenth diamond and a club. Now come the ♣AK and a club ruff with the last trump. East follows three times and West discards a heart. Everyone is left with three hearts and declarer must decide who has the queen. West is known to have started with a 2-4-3-4 shape and East with 2-3-4-4. West is therefore a 4 to 3 favorite to have started with the ♥Q, so declarer cashes the ♥K and successfully finesses the jack to bring home his contract. Declarer played with the odds and was duly rewarded.

At the second table, the contract and the lead are the same. Declarer wins the trump lead and draws a second round. Now come three rounds of diamonds, West following ♦3, ♦6, ♦9 and East ♦2, ♦5, ♦J. Two more rounds of trumps come next, and both defenders part with a heart and a club. Declarer cashes the ♣AK and ruffs the third round of clubs as both defenders follow three times.

When declarer stops to count he knows that both defenders had two spades and four clubs, and were 4-3 in the red suits. Whichever defender has the thirteenth diamond only started with three hearts — but who has the ♦10? There was not much in the fall of the diamonds, but declarer judges that West holds the missing diamond; that means that East began with the four-card heart suit and is, therefore, more likely to hold the queen. Declarer crosses to the ♥A and runs the jack. West produces the ♥Q and the grand slam is one down.

Declarer has no way to find out who has the thirteenth diamond unless a defender tells him by throwing it. There was no legitimate way for declarer to get a sure count of the hand, so he was left with a straight guess (and was perhaps persuaded that West held the long diamond by East's ♦J falsecard on the third round). If you leave declarer with a legitimate 50-50 guess, he will get it wrong half of the time.

Now let's change the defensive hands slightly. If we swap West's ♥Q for one of East's small ones, then the ♥Q is now with the three-card holding. In this case, the last thing the defenders want to do is to leave declarer with a 50-50 guess for the crucial queen. Now it is in the defenders' interests for declarer to get an accurate count since it is likely to lead him to choose the losing option. A very astute declarer may pay you the ultimate compliment of playing against the odds, on the basis that you would not have provided him with a complete count if the percentage play was the winning one. If you meet such a declarer, all we can say is 'don't play against him for money.'

As a final note on this hand, you may have noticed that declarer could have made life tougher for the defenders. Instead of cashing his diamond winners, he should play two more rounds of trumps immediately. Both defenders would have to find two discards and it is far from obvious for both of them to throw a heart and a club. In all likelihood, West will discard a 'useless' small diamond, exposing the distribution when declarer later plays three rounds of that suit.

On the last hand, in order to avoid giving away his distribution a defender had to retain a card declarer could never *force* him to play. Often, you have to discard before you know much about the hand. Most players tend to make the 'easy' discard in this situation, but an alert declarer will often draw the correct inference. Our next hand, which was well played by 'Tosh' MacIntosh in the 1998 British Premier Team League, illustrates the point. Take the South cards:

Neither Vul.
Lead: ♣K

```
              ♠  Q 9 7 3
              ♥  10 5 3
              ◆  A K 4 3
              ♣  A 6

                   N
              W         E
                   S

              ♠  10 8 4
              ♥  A K Q J 7
              ◆  Q 9 8
              ♣  9 5
```

WEST	NORTH	EAST	SOUTH
			1♥
pass	1♠	pass	2♥
pass	4♥	all pass	

You have nine top tricks and your tenth can come either from dummy's long diamond or from establishing a spade trick. However, the club lead leaves you with insufficient time to test both suits. The probability that diamonds are 3-3 is 36%, so on the surface, finessing against the ♠J appears to be a better chance since it is 50%.

You win trick one with the ♣A, but when you begin drawing trumps East discards on the second round. The chances of establishing a spade trick have now been significantly reduced. For a start, West has nine non-hearts to East's twelve, reducing the odds that the the ♠J is onside. You also risk losing trump control. If you draw trumps before playing a spade, even if the ♠J is onside, the defense will win the first spade, cash a club, and force you to use up your last trump with a third round of clubs. When you play a second spade towards dummy, the defense will win and cash club tricks. So, you must play the first round of spades while dummy still has a trump to take care of the third round of clubs.

This means that you need West to hold at least three spades including the jack. If he has ♠Jx, ♠KJ or ♠AJ, West will get a spade ruff in addition to two spade tricks and a club. The chances of establishing a spade trick are, thus, significantly less than 50%. Although neither line of play is a favorite to succeed, the odds seem to weigh marginally in favor of drawing trumps and relying on the diamond suit to produce four tricks.

Before making a decision, there is one important piece of information we have failed to give you. What did East discard on the second round of trumps? The defender at the table was a seasoned international player, but he lazily threw a small diamond. One thing was now virtually certain — diamonds were not originally 3-3. It is inconceivable that East would discard from ♦Jxx in case his partner had ♦Qx. He is also unlikely to have thrown from ♦10xx or ♦xxx when diamonds is obviously a key suit. (Besides, with only four red cards, East would have plenty of useless black cards to throw.) At the table, MacIntosh correctly assumed that East's diamond discard was from a five-card suit. This was the full hand:

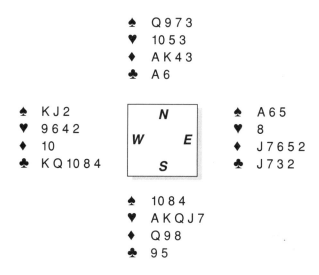

```
              ♠  Q 9 7 3
              ♥  10 5 3
              ♦  A K 4 3
              ♣  A 6

 ♠  K J 2          N           ♠  A 6 5
 ♥  9 6 4 2                    ♥  8
 ♦  10         W       E       ♦  J 7 6 5 2
 ♣  K Q 10 8 4                 ♣  J 7 3 2
                   S

              ♠  10 8 4
              ♥  A K Q J 7
              ♦  Q 9 8
              ♣  9 5
```

Tosh played a spade at trick four and successfully finessed against the jack. On regaining the lead, he drew West's remaining trumps and led a second spade towards dummy to establish the ♠Q as his tenth trick. Had East discarded a club, giving declarer no clues, the contract might well have failed.

Careless discarding is not the only manner in which defenders give away crucial information. An astute declarer learns something about your hand every time you play a card. However, an imaginative defender can sometimes paint a false picture of his hand for declarer:

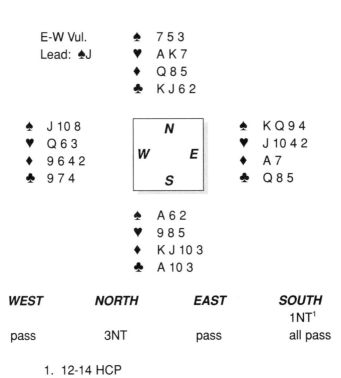

E-W Vul.   ♠ 7 5 3
Lead: ♠J   ♥ A K 7
            ♦ Q 8 5
            ♣ K J 6 2

♠ J 10 8   ♠ K Q 9 4
♥ Q 6 3   ♥ J 10 4 2
♦ 9 6 4 2   ♦ A 7
♣ 9 7 4   ♣ Q 8 5

            ♠ A 6 2
            ♥ 9 8 5
            ♦ K J 10 3
            ♣ A 10 3

WEST	NORTH	EAST	SOUTH
			1NT[1]
pass	3NT	pass	all pass

1. 12-14 HCP

East overtakes the ♠J with the queen, which holds. He then plays king and another spade, declarer winning the third round. When declarer knocks out the ♦A, East declines to cash the long spade, reinforcing the illusion that his partner holds that card. Instead, he simply exits with a diamond.

Look at the hand from declarer's point of view. He has eight top tricks and can easily establish his ninth in clubs. Naturally, he wants to take the club finesse into the safe hand — the one that does not contain the thirteenth spade. Declarer cashes the ♣A and plays a club to dummy's jack. East wins the ♣Q and produces the one card he cannot hold — the last spade. One down!

Was this brilliant defense? Not really. It was just a question of not showing your hand to declarer. There is much truth in the adage 'when defending 3NT, do not take your fourth trick until you can see your fifth.'

It is said that members of the great Italian Blue Team did not play just their own thirteen cards, or even the twenty-six cards belonging to themselves and their partner. They played all fifty-two cards by mentally projecting themselves into the mind of declarer. Watch West at work here to see the benefits of such lateral thinking:

```
E-W Vul.              ♠  A K J 3
Lead: ♦Q              ♥  K Q
                      ♦  5 3
                      ♣  9 7 5 3 2

♠  9 8 5 4 2      ┌─────────────┐      ♠  Q 10 7 6
♥  3              │      N      │      ♥  8 7 5 4 2
♦  Q J 8 4 2      │  W       E  │      ♦  A 6
♣  J 6           │      S      │      ♣  K 4
                 └─────────────┘
                      ♠  —
                      ♥  A J 10 9 6
                      ♦  K 10 9 7
                      ♣  A Q 10 8
```

WEST	NORTH	EAST	SOUTH
			1♥
pass	1♠	pass	2♣
pass	4♣	pass	4♦
pass	4♥	pass	6♣
all pass			

East overtakes the ♦Q and returns a diamond to the king. Declarer crosses to dummy with a heart and plays a trump to the queen. When he cashes the ♣A, the outstanding trumps come tumbling down and declarer is able to claim. That all seems very straightforward, except that at the table things may not go quite that way. Sitting West, you can guess that declarer has ♣AQxx and thus the king and jack are destined to fall under the ace. If only there was some way to persuade declarer to lead another heart before a second round of trumps...

It is only by viewing the hand from declarer's seat that you will spot how he might be pushed into a losing line of play. What do you think declarer will do if you play the ♣J smoothly under the queen? Might he not be convinced that East has ♣Kxx and try to cross back to dummy with a second heart to repeat the trump finesse? When he does, of course, you will be able to ruff with your small trump. A third round of diamonds then allows partner to score the ♣K for two down!

Spectacular? Brilliant? Yes, but any good defender would be disappointed if he missed the play. Playing the jack can never cost. Following with the small club leaves declarer with no option but to cash the ace.

As we have seen previously, when one defender has most of his side's assets, he is susceptible to being endplayed or squeezed. Some squeezes, like the one overleaf, work automatically and offer the defense no chance to cloud the issue:

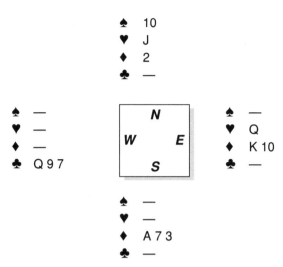

You are South, playing notrump, and the lead is in dummy. When you play dummy's spade, East cannot keep both the master heart and the diamond stopper. Provided you have been watching the hearts, you will know whether dummy's ♥J is good. It would make no difference if the East and West hands were switched. It will always be clear which red suit to play at trick twelve.

However, there are hands on which a squeeze has worked but declarer must still read the position to reap the reward. Watch what happens on this deal:

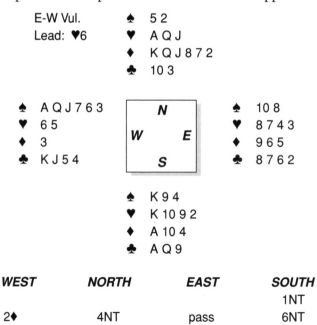

WEST	NORTH	EAST	SOUTH
			1NT
2♦	4NT	pass	6NT
all pass			

South opens a 15-17 1NT and West's 2♦ shows spades and another suit. North makes a quantitative notrump raise and South, with his good intermediates, accepts. The heart lead gives nothing away, and declarer can see eleven top tricks. It is highly probable that both the ♠A and the ♣K are offside, so it is not possible for him to lose one early trick without losing a second. The only hope is a strip squeeze.

After cashing dummy's heart honors, declarer crosses to the ♦A, discards a club on the ♥K and then runs off another four rounds of diamonds to reach this ending:

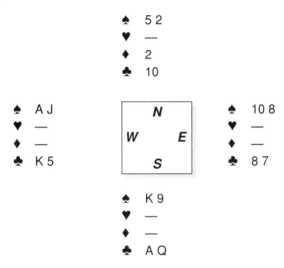

On the last diamond, declarer throws his small spade. If West agonizes over his discard and eventually parts with the ♠J, declarer will have little trouble endplaying him with his now-bare ♠A to lead away from the ♣K. Similarly, if he pitches a club then declarer plays a club to the ace, felling the king, and again the slam is made. Even if West manages to convey the impression that his final discard is as painless as a stroll in the park, declarer is likely to play for him to have come down to the last four cards shown above.

The contract is, in fact, unbeatable, but that does not mean that East-West should pack up and go home. If West is a counting defender, he will see this end position coming well in advance. The secret of successful defense against this type of ending is to make your difficult discards early. Let's say West keeps ♠AJ6 and the ♣K as his last four cards. The impression he is trying to create in declarer's mind is that his original shape was 5-2-1-5 rather than his actual 6-2-1-4. When West now throws the ♠J on the last diamond, might not declarer misread what has happened and attempt to endplay him with his presumed-singleton ♠A?

As a final word on this hand, it is worth noting that East's play is far from irrelevant to the success of this defense. It is imperative that he keeps cards in both black suits to avoid exposing West's deception. He must also avoid signalling his black-suit lengths, as this may also tip declarer off.

LESSONS FROM THIS CHAPTER

- Don't show declarer your hand!

- Don't show declarer your hand!

- Guard the shape of your hand jealously. Avoid providing declarer with gratuitous information that he cannot obtain on his own.

- If a count of declarer's tricks, shape and points tells you that the contract is destined to succeed, look for a way to provide declarer with a losing option by painting a false picture of your hand.

- When discarding, do not just consider which card is the safest, but also which one gives declarer the least information.

- Do not signal before considering who is most likely to benefit from the information.

- Did we mention 'don't show declarer your hand'?

CHAPTER 17

Concealing Your Honors

In the last chapter, we saw how defenders can protect their honors by concealing the distribution of their hands. Thoughtful management of the defense's high cards is also important. For example, if you pass as dealer and then show up with an ace and two kings in the first few tricks, there is no chance that an alert declarer will play you for a crucial queen. Conversely, if the opponents bid to game after you have passed an eleven-count, it may be advantageous to let declarer see most of your high cards early. Later in the play, he will be more inclined to misguess, playing your partner for a vital jack or queen that you also hold.

Even if declarer knows from the bidding which defender has most of the high cards, it may still be possible to mislead him as to the position of a key honor. Our first example occurred in a pairs event, where the allure of a precious overtrick often tempts greedy declarers. If you feel ready to perpetrate a little sandbagging, take the West seat and cover the East and South cards:

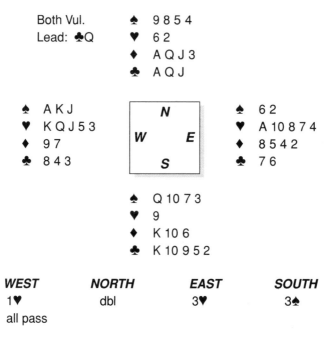

Both Vul.
Lead: ♣Q

	♠ 9 8 5 4	
	♥ 6 2	
	♦ A Q J 3	
	♣ A Q J	

♠ A K J		♠ 6 2
♥ K Q J 5 3		♥ A 10 8 7 4
♦ 9 7		♦ 8 5 4 2
♣ 8 4 3		♣ 7 6

	♠ Q 10 7 3	
	♥ 9	
	♦ K 10 6	
	♣ K 10 9 5 2	

WEST	NORTH	EAST	SOUTH
1♥	dbl	3♥	3♠
all pass			

You lead a top heart. Partner plays the ♥4 (showing an odd number of hearts) and declarer follows with the nine. What is your plan?

You can already count the whole hand. Partner has ♥A10xxx, and having made a preemptive raise to 3♥, he will not also have an outside king. Declarer's minor suits are therefore solid. You can see one heart and three trump tricks, but there is no legitimate chance of a fifth defensive trick. That's no reason to give up though. Perhaps declarer can be persuaded that he has a chance for an overtrick. You play a second heart which declarer ruffs, as expected. After crossing to dummy with a club, declarer runs the ♠9 to your... king!

With no losers to throw, a ruff and discard cannot help declarer so you continue with a third round of hearts. If declarer ruffs in the South hand, he will no longer be able to finesse against East's presumed ♠J; he therefore ruffs in dummy. When he repeats the trump finesse, you win your jack, draw the remaining trumps with the ace, and cash the hearts to beat the contract by two.

This declarer knew only that West had an opening bid, so it was entirely possible that the ♠J was onside. If your high card strength is known within fairly narrow limits, you may have to work harder to portray a false picture of your hand. On our next exhibit, East has opened with a revealing 15-17 1NT:

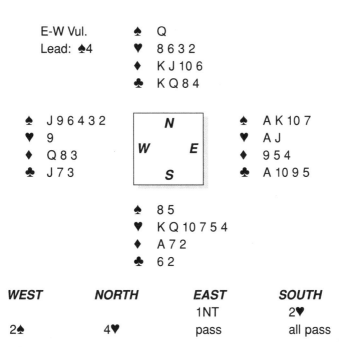

E-W Vul.
Lead: ♠4

♠	Q
♥	8 6 3 2
♦	K J 10 6
♣	K Q 8 4

West	East
♠ J 9 6 4 3 2	♠ A K 10 7
♥ 9	♥ A J
♦ Q 8 3	♦ 9 5 4
♣ J 7 3	♣ A 10 9 5

♠	8 5
♥	K Q 10 7 5 4
♦	A 7 2
♣	6 2

WEST	NORTH	EAST	SOUTH
		1NT	2♥
2♠	4♥	pass	all pass

You are East, and partner leads the ♠4. if you automatically win the first trick with the ♠K, the defense is effectively dead. Let's say you switch to the ace and jack of trumps. A club is played to the king and you have to take your ace. Declarer has now 'seen' sixteen points in your hand. Because your 1NT was limited to seventeen he will have little trouble finessing your partner for the ♦Q and bringing home his game.

If, instead, you win trick one with the ♠A, perhaps even gilding the lily by returning a small spade to partner's known jack, declarer is likely to place West with the ♠K. He will then 'know' that you have the ♦Q and he will misguess the diamonds. One down!

The next hand features a classic deceptive play:

N-S Vul.
Lead: ♠9

```
                    ♠  7 6 3
                    ♥  A Q J
                    ♦  K 10 9
                    ♣  A K J 5

♠  9 4                               ♠  K Q 8 5 2
♥  K 9 7 5 2        N                ♥  6 4
♦  8 4 2         W     E             ♦  A Q 7 3
♣  9 6 4                             ♣  7 3
                    S

                    ♠  A J 10
                    ♥  10 8 3
                    ♦  J 6 5
                    ♣  Q 10 8 2
```

WEST	NORTH	EAST	SOUTH
		1♠	pass
pass	dbl	pass	1NT
pass	3NT	all pass	

Again you are East. As partner is unlikely to regain the lead, there is no point in ducking the first trick so you play the ♠Q. Declarer takes the ace and immediately plays a diamond to dummy's ten. Declarer knows you have the ♦A. If you win the first diamond with the queen, he has no choice but to rely on finding the ♥K onside. However, if you smoothly win the first round of diamonds with the ace, is there not a good chance that declarer will rely on repeating the 'proven' diamond finesse for his contract?

On this hand, having opened the bidding, you could not disguise the fact that you had most of the defense's high cards. All you could do was give declarer a legitimate losing option. The next hand offers another example of 'playing the card you are known to hold':

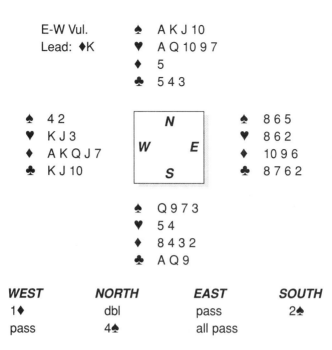

```
E-W Vul.          ♠ A K J 10
Lead: ♦K          ♥ A Q 10 9 7
                  ♦ 5
                  ♣ 5 4 3

♠ 4 2            N            ♠ 8 6 5
♥ K J 3                       ♥ 8 6 2
♦ A K Q J 7    W     E        ♦ 10 9 6
♣ K J 10          S           ♣ 8 7 6 2

                  ♠ Q 9 7 3
                  ♥ 5 4
                  ♦ 8 4 3 2
                  ♣ A Q 9
```

WEST	NORTH	EAST	SOUTH
1♦	dbl	pass	2♠
pass	4♠	all pass	

As West, you lead a top diamond and continue with a second round of the suit to force dummy. Declarer cashes the ♠A, overtakes the ♠J with his queen, and finesses dummy's ♥Q. Next comes the ♥A.

Declarer knows you have the ♥K. If you follow woodenly with the jack he will know it is safe to to ruff the third round of hearts. With the suit breaking 3-3, he will make ten tricks in comfort. If, instead, you play the ♥K (the card you are known to hold) under dummy's ace, you at least give declarer a choice. He may decide to run the ♥10, playing you for two major-suit doubletons. If he does, you will get a chance to force dummy with a third round of diamonds, effectively killing the heart suit.

Be aware that declarer gains information on every trick. The only way to prevent him from learning anything new is to play a card he already knows you have. This theme can be seen in numerous suit combinations. Look at the heart suit on the next deal:

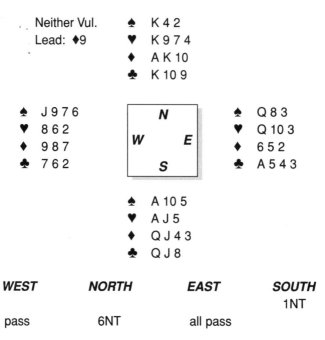

Neither Vul.
Lead: ♦9

North hand:
♠ K 4 2
♥ K 9 7 4
♦ A K 10
♣ K 10 9

West hand:
♠ J 9 7 6
♥ 8 6 2
♦ 9 8 7
♣ 7 6 2

East hand:
♠ Q 8 3
♥ Q 10 3
♦ 6 5 2
♣ A 5 4 3

South hand:
♠ A 10 5
♥ A J 5
♦ Q J 4 3
♣ Q J 8

WEST	NORTH	EAST	SOUTH
			1NT
pass	6NT	all pass	

North's nines and tens convince him to do more than just invite a slam. Declarer wins the diamond lead and immediately runs four rounds of the suit, both defenders and dummy discarding clubs. A club is played to the king and you, as East, win the ace and return the suit. Declarer plays a spade to the king and a heart to the jack. He now cashes the ♥A and if you do not follow smoothly with the queen, the card you are known to hold, declarer will have no choice but to follow the winning line of playing for hearts to break 3-3. Assuming you have played the queen on the second round of hearts, these cards remain:

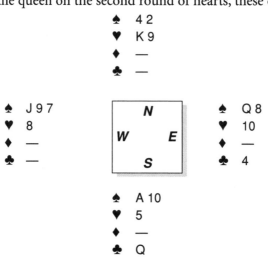

North hand:
♠ 4 2
♥ K 9
♦ —
♣ —

West hand:
♠ J 9 7
♥ 8
♦ —
♣ —

East hand:
♠ Q 8
♥ 10
♦ —
♣ 4

South hand:
♠ A 10
♥ 5
♦ —
♣ Q

Aware that East's ♥Q may have been a falsecard, declarer attempts to get a count on the majors. He takes his club winner on which West, who is alert to declarer's problem, discards a spade. When the ♠A is cashed, West follows with the jack. A heart is led towards dummy at Trick 12 and West produces the ♥8. The odds are that declarer will misguess by finessing dummy's nine. Always bear in mind that if you defend in such a way that declarer has two believable alternatives, he will frequently guess wrong.

Sometimes it seems that declarer is destined to succeed. Consider this trump position:

Dummy
♣ 10 9 6 4

Declarer
♣ A K 8 5 2

You are declarer, as South, and this is your trump suit. West leads the ♣3, East plays the queen, and you win. Do you lay down the other top honor and hope the suit breaks 2-2, or do you cross to dummy and finesse against East's presumed ♣QJx? Most declarers will choose to play for ♣QJx on their right.

As a defender on opening lead, you can sometimes judge from the bidding that declarer has a nine-card trump fit and that most of the high cards are on your right. In these cases, you will often generate a trick from nothing by leading a small trump from Jx or, even more spectacular when it works, from Qx. Even if declarer gets it right, at least you will have provided him with a losing option, which is often the best you can do.

This point is emphasized by our final hand, which comes from the 1998 Pan Asian Bridge Federation Championships. The defense could not give declarer a legitimate way to go down, but any losing option is better than none. Sometimes declarer will leap, lemming-like, into the abyss:

```
Both Vul.        ♠  J 7 5 3
Lead: ♠Q         ♥  9 5
                 ♦  K J 9 2
                 ♣  A K 3

♠  Q 9              N          ♠  A K 10 8
♥  Q J 7 3                     ♥  10 8 6
♦  Q 10 7      W       E       ♦  6 4
♣  J 10 6 2         S          ♣  9 7 5 4

                 ♠  6 4 2
                 ♥  A K 4 2
                 ♦  A 8 5 3
                 ♣  Q 8
```

WEST	NORTH	EAST	SOUTH
			1♦
pass	1♠	pass	1NT
pass	2NT	pass	3NT
pass	pass	dbl	all pass

West, Ben Thompson of Australia, led the ♠Q and a second spade to East's ten. When declarer followed to the third spade (meaning the defense had only four spade tricks) things looked bleak from the West seat. Thompson could account for all of the high cards, as declarer must have the remaining thirteen points for his opening bid and his acceptance of the game try. With the diamonds lying well for declarer, legitimate defensive prospects were non-existent. The only chance for the defense was to persuade declarer that East's double was based on more than just ♠AK10x.

Working on the basis that if you can find a losing option to offer declarer, just occasionally he will take it, Thompson discarded a heart on the third spade and the ♦10 on the fourth! Declarer duly won the heart switch, played a diamond to dummy's king and ran the ♦J to West's queen. Unbelievable perhaps, but true!

- Be aware of approximately how declarer will expect the defensive high cards to be distributed based on the bidding.

- To persuade declarer to play you for an honor you don't have, conceal a high card in another suit.

- Play the card you are known to hold.

- Conceal your high cards in such a way that declarer will choose a finesse that is losing rather than one that is working.

- Defend in a way that leaves declarer with a *believable* alternative to the winning line of play.

- If you can see that declarer is fated to succeed, look for *any* way to offer him a losing option.

CHAPTER 18

Making Declarer Decide Early

We have seen how concealing your distribution and the location of the defensive honors can cause declarer to choose a losing option. Defenders can also bend the odds in their favor by forcing declarer to make a critical decision before he has had time to gather all of the available information.

Good declarers prefer to combine their options rather than risk all or nothing on one chance. It therefore stands to reason that passively allowing declarer to test each option in turn is not in your interest. Suppose declarer has two chances of making a contract — a 3-3 break in one suit or, failing that, a finesse in another suit. If you force him into an early decision in the finesse suit, before he has time to test the second suit, you reduce his options from two to one. He must decide immediately which basket to use for all of his eggs.

These positions occur in many forms. Given that clue, perhaps you feel ready to test your defense. If so, cover the West and South hands and take over from East defending against a slam on this first deal.

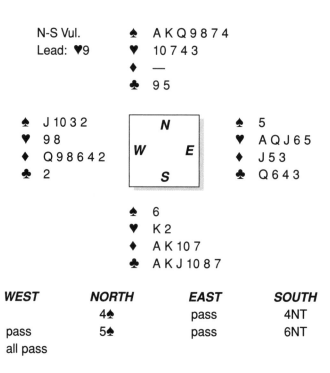

	N-S Vul.	♠	A K Q 9 8 7 4
	Lead: ♥9	♥	10 7 4 3
		♦	—
		♣	9 5

West:
♠ J 10 3 2
♥ 9 8
♦ Q 9 8 6 4 2
♣ 2

East:
♠ 5
♥ A Q J 6 5
♦ J 5 3
♣ Q 6 4 3

South:
♠ 6
♥ K 2
♦ A K 10 7
♣ A K J 10 8 7

WEST	NORTH	EAST	SOUTH
	4♠	pass	4NT
pass	5♠	pass	6NT
all pass			

South's 4NT is Roman Key Card Blackwood and North's response confirms the three top spades. South chooses the notrump slam to protect his heart holding. Sitting East, you win the heart lead with the ace. What do you return?

You have no clear picture of the South hand. If he has two or more spades, he will doubtless claim his contract in a moment or two. But what if he has only one spade? Think about how the play might go if you return a heart. It seems that declarer will win the ♥K and play a spade. When he discovers he has only three tricks in that suit, he will lead the ♣9 from dummy and run it. A second club finesse will then pick up your queen. Declarer is destined to succeed despite the poor breaks. Can you see a way to spike his guns?

You know that when spades fail to break declarer will need to make minor-suit tricks. Your only constructive return at this point is a club, to force him into a premature decision in the suit that may be his alternative source of tricks. Do you think declarer will stake his contract on the club finesse when a 3-2 spade break will give him twelve top tricks? Of course not. He will play the ♣K and cash the top spades. Now, when spades do not break, he will only be able to take one club finesse — not enough to pick up your queen.

Now that you have the idea, try this problem:

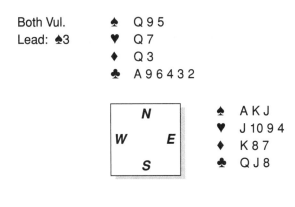

Both Vul.
Lead: ♠3

```
          ♠ Q 9 5
          ♥ Q 7
          ♦ Q 3
          ♣ A 9 6 4 3 2
                              ♠ A K J
                              ♥ J 10 9 4
                              ♦ K 8 7
                              ♣ Q J 8
```

WEST	NORTH	EAST	SOUTH
			1NT
pass	3NT	all pass	

South's 1NT shows 15-17, so you know exactly how many points your partner has — zero! How do you plan to defend?

You know that declarer has the ♥AK, ♣K and ♦AJ. What is his distribution? Partner's lead suggests five spades, leaving only a doubleton for declarer. Almost certainly, he has at least three clubs. You cannot prevent declarer from establishing nine tricks, so you have to find five defensive tricks quickly. You can count three spades and a club, and your only hope for a fifth trick is the ♦K.

What do you think will happen if you win ♠J, cash the ♠AK, and switch to a diamond at Trick 4? This is the full hand:

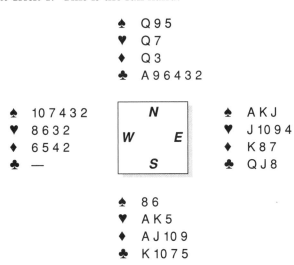

```
               ♠ Q 9 5
               ♥ Q 7
               ♦ Q 3
               ♣ A 9 6 4 3 2

  ♠ 10 7 4 3 2                    ♠ A K J
  ♥ 8 6 3 2                       ♥ J 10 9 4
  ♦ 6 5 4 2                       ♦ K 8 7
  ♣ —                             ♣ Q J 8

               ♠ 8 6
               ♥ A K 5
               ♦ A J 10 9
               ♣ K 10 7 5
```

Put yourself in declarer's position. With a ten-card club fit, he can claim the remaining tricks if the suit breaks 2-1. Will he take the diamond finesse and risk letting West in to cash his spades? If you know a declarer who would, perhaps we could persuade him to play some high-stakes rubber bridge... Of course, a rational declarer will play the ♦A — and when West shows out on the first club there will be no way to recover.

The defense succeeded on these first two deals because declarer refused what appeared to be an unnecessary finesse. Another way to restrict declarer's options is to force him to make a premature discard:

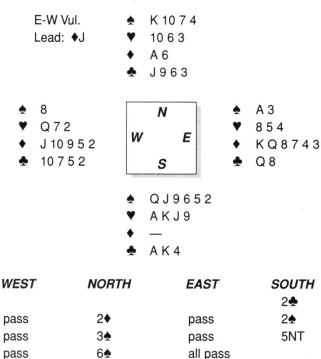

		E-W Vul.		♠ K 10 7 4	
		Lead: ♦J		♥ 10 6 3	
				♦ A 6	
				♣ J 9 6 3	

♠ 8   ♠ A 3
♥ Q 7 2   ♥ 8 5 4
♦ J 10 9 5 2 ♦ K Q 8 7 4 3
♣ 10 7 5 2   ♣ Q 8

♠ Q J 9 6 5 2
♥ A K J 9
♦ —
♣ A K 4

WEST	NORTH	EAST	SOUTH
			2♣
pass	2♦	pass	2♠
pass	3♠	pass	5NT
pass	6♠	all pass	

After his spades are raised, South asks about trump honors and settles for the small slam on discovering that a top trump is missing. Declarer plays dummy's small diamond on the first trick and ruffs in hand. Sitting East, you win the second trick with the ♠A, partner following. How should you defend?

It looks tempting to play a heart through. Alternatively, you could exit safely with a second round of trumps? Even looking at the full hand it may seem that it does not matter what you do. Indeed, declarer can always make the hand but, of course, he doesn't know your ♣Q is coming down doubleton. Let's say you return a second diamond to dummy's bare ace. What do you think declarer will discard? In his shoes, wouldn't you discard the club loser and take your chances on finding either the ♣Q10 doubleton or the heart finesse working?

If you return a heart instead, declarer will win, draw the last trump, and cash the ♣AK. When the queen falls, he will finesse against West's ♣10. The ♣J and ♦A will then provide discards for declarer's two heart losers. Returning a spade leads to the same position. However, if you force declarer to make his discard before he knows what to throw, he will sometimes do the wrong thing.

The next hand is a tougher example of the same principle, but counting should enable the East player to get right. If it's not too late in the day, cover the West and South hands and plan the defense from the East seat.

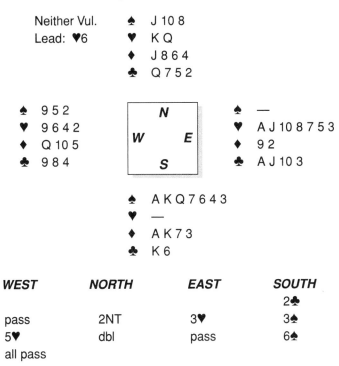

Neither Vul.
Lead: ♥6

North:
♠ J 10 8
♥ K Q
♦ J 8 6 4
♣ Q 7 5 2

West:
♠ 9 5 2
♥ 9 6 4 2
♦ Q 10 5
♣ 9 8 4

East:
♠ —
♥ A J 10 8 7 5 3
♦ 9 2
♣ A J 10 3

South:
♠ A K Q 7 6 4 3
♥ —
♦ A K 7 3
♣ K 6

WEST	NORTH	EAST	SOUTH
			2♣
pass	2NT	3♥	3♠
5♥	dbl	pass	6♠
all pass			

Many defenders in the East seat would let the contract through before they even started to think about the hand. West has found the only lead to beat the hand so how should you defend, and why?

Sitting East, you can tell from partner's jump raise that he holds four hearts, and so you know that declarer is void. If you cover dummy's ♥K with the ace, declarer will ruff and take his discard at leisure, later in the play. Holding off your ♥A at Trick 1 forces declarer to decide what to discard immediately. On this hand, that will make the difference between 6♠ making and going down!

Let's see what happens if you cover dummy's heart immediately. Declarer will ruff, cash a top spade and play a second spade to dummy. When he leads a low club, what can you do? You are caught in a Morton's Fork. If you win the

♣A, declarer has two winners (the ♣Q and the ♥Q) on which to park his losing diamonds. On the other hand, if you duck your ♣A, he will win the ♣K, draw the last trump with dummy's jack, discard his club loser on the ♥Q and concede a diamond.

Look at the difference if you let the ♥K hold at trick one. What should declarer discard? The answer is that it doesn't matter what he throws, he's down one. You cannot stop declarer from taking a discard on dummy's heart, but you can make him do so at an inconvenient moment rather than when it suits him.

Our final example on the subject of forcing declarer to make a decision before he is ready to, concerns the trump suit. Most defenders would solve the problem on this next hand by counting their potential defensive tricks:

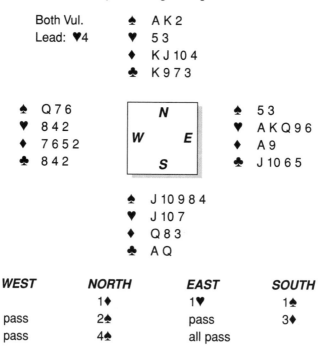

Both Vul.   ♠ A K 2
Lead: ♥4   ♥ 5 3
    ♦ K J 10 4
    ♣ K 9 7 3

♠ Q 7 6   ♠ 5 3
♥ 8 4 2   ♥ A K Q 9 6
♦ 7 6 5 2   ♦ A 9
♣ 8 4 2   ♣ J 10 6 5

    ♠ J 10 9 8 4
    ♥ J 10 7
    ♦ Q 8 3
    ♣ A Q

WEST	NORTH	EAST	SOUTH
	1♦	1♥	1♠
pass	2♠	pass	3♦
pass	4♠	all pass	

South's 1♠ bid shows at least a five-card suit and his 3♦ is a game try. With a maximum for the auction so far, North accepts.

Sitting East, you win the ♥Q at Trick 1. You cash the king next, and partner follows with the ♥8, so you know that both South and West started with three hearts. The ♦A will be the defense's third trick, but declarer must have most of the remaining twelve points for his game try facing a minimum-range opening bid. Is there any chance?

If you are to beat the contract, West must have a useful honor. He cannot have the missing ace. South's 3♦ bid suggests that he has the ♦Q, and in any case, if that is partner's honor then declarer is virtually certain to guess the suit correctly after your overcall. Neither will the ♣Q in partner's hand be of any use; declarer only has five minor-suit cards and any club loser will be discarded on dummy's diamonds. The only chance is that West has the ♠Qxx. If he does, you can promote a trump trick for him by leading your third heart honor.

On this layout, the defenders can promote a trump trick by force. On other occasions, you can only restrict declarer's options in the trump suit. Look at this familiar trump position:

Dummy
♣ K 7 4

Declarer
♣ A Q 10 6 5

Any competent declarer knows that the correct way to handle this suit is to cash the ace and then cross to the king. If West shows out, you are in dummy to take the marked finesse against East. Declarer plays the suit for no losers whenever it breaks 3-2 or when East has ♣Jxxx. What happens when the defenders make dummy ruff, though? Now most declarers will simply cash the king and lead small to the ace, hoping for a 3-2 break. When East has ♣Jxxx, he is likely to get a trump trick.

Then again, if the defenders go out of their way to force dummy to ruff, should declarer play the king and then finesse the ten? Maybe some declarers would take this line, drawing the inference that the defense must have some reason for forcing dummy. All we can say is that when defending against such declarers, be sure to make every effort to force dummy whenever West's trumps could be Jx or Jxx.

The concept of removing declarer's options comes in numerous guises. If you like, cover the East and South cards and try to solve West's defensive problem on the next exhibit.

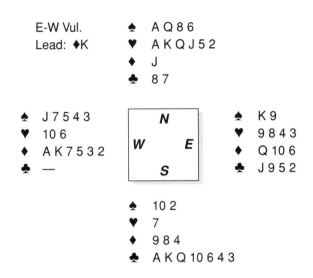

E-W Vul.
Lead: ♦K

North: ♠ A Q 8 6 ♥ A K Q J 5 2 ♦ J ♣ 8 7

West: ♠ J 7 5 4 3 ♥ 10 6 ♦ A K 7 5 3 2 ♣ —

East: ♠ K 9 ♥ 9 8 4 3 ♦ Q 10 6 ♣ J 9 5 2

South: ♠ 10 2 ♥ 7 ♦ 9 8 4 ♣ A K Q 10 6 4 3

WEST	NORTH	EAST	SOUTH
			3NT
pass	4♦	pass	4♥
pass	5♦	pass	6♣
all pass			

South's 3NT opening is 'Gambling', showing a solid minor suit. North's 4♦ asks if South has a singleton and 4♥ shows shortness. 5♦ is 'Pass or Correct' — South is expected to pass if diamonds is his suit or correct to 6♣, as here. You lead the ♦K, requesting count, and partner plays the six. What now?

If declarer's trumps are solid, he will be able to claim his contract, whatever you play next. You must therefore assume that his trumps are ♣AKQ10xxx, leaving partner with ♣Jxxx. If you continue with a second high diamond, forcing dummy to ruff, declarer will be forced to take an immediate view in the trump suit. Doubtless he will make the normal (but, on this occasion, losing) decision to play the suit from the top.

If you play anything but a diamond, the contract will succeed. Many defenders would try a spade, but declarer will rise with the ace and cross to the trump ace, discovering the bad break. He can then return to dummy with a heart, throw three losers on the hearts (your partner following impotently), and take the marked finesse in trumps. Perhaps you think declarer should figure out to take a trump finesse once you force dummy. You'll enjoy that next time — when you hold jack doubleton in the trump suit!

On the next deal, declarer has a 50-50 guess in the trump suit, with a small slam at stake. Have a quick look at all four hands and see if you think he will guess right after a club lead.

```
                N-S Vul.        ♠  K J 9 3 2
                Lead: ♣10       ♥  K 6 5 2
                                ♦  7
                                ♣  K Q J

      ♠  7 6 4              N              ♠  8 5
      ♥  4                                 ♥  Q 8 7 3
      ♦  J 9 6 3     W            E        ♦  K 8 4
      ♣  10 9 7 4 3            S           ♣  A 8 6 2

                                ♠  A Q 10
                                ♥  A J 10 9
                                ♦  A Q 10 5 2
                                ♣  5
```

WEST	NORTH	EAST	SOUTH
			1♦
pass	1♠	pass	2♥
pass	3♣	pass	3♠
pass	4♥	pass	6♥
all pass			

Do you think declarer will succeed? Against most defenders the answer
would be, 'No idea — it's a complete guess, isn't it?' At the table, however, East
found a way to make it almost certain that declarer would go wrong. After winning the diamond lead he switched to the three of trumps!

Declarer could not believe that anyone would switch to a trump from the
queen. He put in the jack, which won, then cashed the ace of trumps. His face
when West showed out was a sight to be remembered!

LESSONS FROM THIS CHAPTER

- Force declarer to take or refuse a finesse before he knows whether
  or not he needs it for his contract.

- Force declarer to make discards before he knows what to throw.

- Look to reduce declarer's options in the trump suit. Forcing the short
  trump hand to ruff is one way to achieve this objective.

CHAPTER 19

True or False? When to Play Honest Cards

Often you can see that declarer will be forced into a winning line of play unless you can offer him a plausible alternative. In this closing chapter, we introduce numerous situations in which a count of the hand suggests that a smokescreen is needed. When a count of declarer's tricks tells you the contract is destined to make, desperate measures are called for. Fortunately, there are many strategies you can employ.

We begin with the question of signalling. When should you send an honest message and when should you set out to mislead declarer? Obviously, if you always signal honestly, declarer will have an easy time counting your shape. Similarly, if you religiously signal partner whenever you have an honor, declarer will have little trouble guessing which finesse to take.

Having said that, we strongly believe that your basic philosophy should be to signal accurately if there is any chance that not doing so will cause partner to go wrong. If you cannot rely on the accuracy of one another's signals, partnership confidence will be materially damaged. When you reach the point in the hand at which a crucial decision must be made, you should always base your defense on the assumption that partner has provided you with reliable information. Doing anything else reduces defense to guesswork, and the resulting errors will cost far more than will ever be lost through declarers using your honest defensive signals to their advantage.

Here is a simple partnership rule that is worth adopting: *if it is likely that partner needs accurate information, signal honestly.*

Curiously, it is against slams, when accurate defense is vital, that you often hear players make a comment such as, 'I didn't signal because I didn't want to give away the position.' Our first deal demonstrates this principle. Few East players would appreciate their critical role in the defense of this hand:

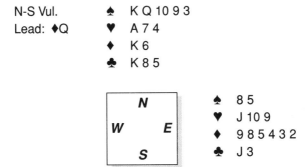

	♠	K Q 10 9 3
N-S Vul.	♥	A 7 4
Lead: ♦Q	♦	K 6
	♣	K 8 5

♠ 8 5
♥ J 10 9
♦ 9 8 5 4 3 2
♣ J 3

WEST	NORTH	EAST	SOUTH
			1NT
pass	2♥[1]	pass	2♠
pass	4NT	pass	6♠
all pass			

1. Transfer

Everyone will be familiar with this scenario. You pick up the East hand and find yourself with a boring two-count. You hear LHO open a strong notrump, and your mind starts to wander. As the opponents conduct a strong auction, you force yourself to concentrate long enough to notice that you are not going to be on lead. You then return to thoughts about where to go to eat after the game, what you have to do tomorrow, and so on.

Finally, the opponents stop bidding. Partner leads the ♦Q and it registers that your side has no diamond trick and no trump trick. Your hearts might be important if partner has an honor so, having little else, you decide to cling grimly to them.

It occurs to you that declarer will not be able to tell how the diamonds are breaking and might miscount the hand, so you follow with the ♦2 under dummy's king at Trick 1. Declarer leads a spade from dummy and you follow suit. You follow again to the second trump, as does partner. When declarer plays a third trump, partner thinks for a while; your mind wanders to what sort of game you are having and then moves on to a new project you are starting at work next week. It's your turn to play and you throw the ♦3 on the third trump. Perhaps it registers that partner has thrown a heart. Declarer plays another trump...

Partner is about to let the contract through by discarding a club. At the end of the hand you will no doubt commiserate that it wasn't easy for him to know what to throw. Here is the full hand:

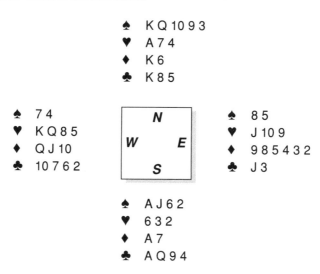

```
                    ♠  K Q 10 9 3
                    ♥  A 7 4
                    ♦  K 6
                    ♣  K 8 5

  ♠  7 4            ┌──────────┐       ♠  8 5
  ♥  K Q 8 5        │    N     │       ♥  J 10 9
  ♦  Q J 10         │ W      E │       ♦  9 8 5 4 3 2
  ♣  10 7 6 2       │    S     │       ♣  J 3
                    └──────────┘

                    ♠  A J 6 2
                    ♥  6 3 2
                    ♦  A 7
                    ♣  A Q 9 4
```

Now, consider how you could have beaten this slam. The first thing that should strike you is that your partner has most of the defensive assets, a fact that should immediately set off alarm bells. He will need you to tell him what is going on as early in the hand as possible. At trick one you must signal your length accurately by playing a high diamond. Do not play the ♦4 or the ♦5 and leave him to work out if it is a low card or a high card. Play the ♦8 — second highest from an even number (playing the ♦9 might be read as a suit-preference signal and your hearts are not good enough for that).

Your hearts are the only significant feature of your hand, and this is information partner will be grateful to hear. When declarer leads a trump at trick two, play the ♠8 as a suit-preference signal. (When you discard on the third round of trumps, partner will understand that your high-low was a suit-preference signal rather than some kind of trump signal.)

When declarer cashes the third round of trumps, discard the ♦2. The precise meaning of this will depend on what specific signals you have agreed with your partner, but our preference is to play high-low with your second and third highest cards (if you can afford them) to show exactly four. Therefore, whenever partner sees the lowest missing card in the suit as the second half of your high-low, he knows you started with either two or six.

All West needs to know to beat this slam is that you have six diamonds and some help in hearts. Declarer plays a fourth trump, on which partner now comfortably throws a diamond. Then declarer plays the ♦A and ducks a heart. Partner wins the ♥Q as you follow with the jack (confirming possession of the ten), and exits with a heart to dummy's ace. When declarer cashes dummy's last trump, you throw another diamond and partner knows he can safely discard the ♥K.

These are the last four cards:

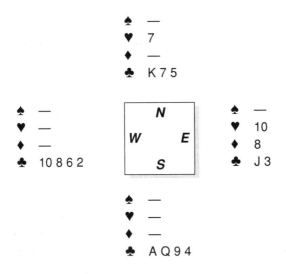

The defenders will come to a second trick and the slam will go down. Without your help, what do you think are partner's chances of knowing that he must keep his four clubs and throw everything else?

This is not to say that as a defender you should blindly signal throughout every hand. There will be many times when you can judge that the information is likely to be of use only to declarer. On the last hand, it was imperative for you to give count so that partner knew which suit he could afford to unguard. Giving count when declarer plays on a suit may help partner know when to hold up an ace, for example. It is easy to overdo it though. Indeed, giving a count signal can be positively dangerous in some situations. Look at this suit.

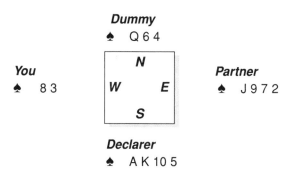

Dummy
♠ Q 6 4

You
♠ 8 3

Partner
♠ J 9 7 2

Declarer
♠ A K 10 5

Declarer plays the ace and crosses to the queen. The odds here favor playing the king next rather than taking a finesse, but only very slightly. If West follows with the ♠8 then the ♠3, declarer might buck the odds and take a winning view, especially if he knows West is a fanatical count signaller. Entries permitting, declarer does best to lead to the queen on the first round — this dramatically increases the chances that West will give an honest length signal.

Having begun this chapter with a hand emphasizing the importance of accurate signalling, we now move on to situations in which a little larceny can produce a windfall. When you know that partner cannot do the wrong thing you have a 'license to mislead'. Maybe he has ♥KQJ10xx and a collection of small cards. He just has to avoid throwing his hearts, and he doesn't need you to tell him that. Alternatively, perhaps you can count that partner has no high cards, and thus you know he can never gain the lead and has no honors to unguard. In short, he has the hand that is sometimes marked in diagrams as 'Irrelevant'. Clearly, in these situations there is no point in you signalling for any purpose other than to lead declarer astray.

The corollary to this is that when you have nothing or very little, as on the hand above, you must be sure to signal your count accurately, particularly early in the hand. Almost certainly, partner will have to make a critical decision. He may need to know how he can exit safely or which suit to discard. It is vital that,when you hold the weak hand, you provide the information needed so that your partner will consistently get these decisions right.

Say the opposition bid 1NT-3NT. One defender has an opening bid and the other almost nothing. The strong hand can falsecard to mislead declarer if he considers it appropriate, whereas the weak hand must signal accurately, at least early in the hand. Declarer may know that one defender is signalling accurately and the other is not, but he will not be able to tell who is lying. However, both defenders will know exactly what is going on.

It is seldom right to falsecard on the opening lead. Having said that, there are those occasions just discussed when you know partner has little or nothing. In such circumstances, a little subterfuge is unlikely to cost and may pay handsome dividends:

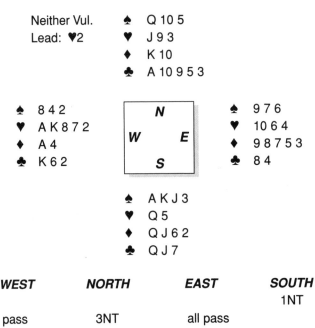

Neither Vul.
Lead: ♥2

♠	Q 10 5
♥	J 9 3
♦	K 10
♣	A 10 9 5 3

♠	8 4 2
♥	A K 8 7 2
♦	A 4
♣	K 6 2

♠	9 7 6
♥	10 6 4
♦	9 8 7 5 3
♣	8 4

♠	A K J 3
♥	Q 5
♦	Q J 6 2
♣	Q J 7

WEST	NORTH	EAST	SOUTH
			1NT
pass	3NT	all pass	

South's 1NT shows 15-17 points. As West, how many high cards do you expect partner to have? Even playing fourth-highest leads, it can never cost to lead the ♥2. It matters not a hoot that partner might be misled, since all he is going to do is to play a succession of small cards. Consider the hand from declarer's viewpoint — it appears that hearts are 4-4. Doesn't it look right to establish nine tricks by knocking out the ♦A rather than risk setting up a fifth defensive trick by taking the club finesse?

On the normal ♥7 lead, although West could have something like ♥AK87 or ♥87xx, declarer will probably decide that the club finesse offers a better chance than a 4-4 heart break. As a final point, it is worth mentioning that if West holds ♥AK72 he might gain by leading the ♥7, pretending that he has a five-card suit. Such a lead might encourage declarer to take a losing finesse rather than to knock out an ace. When you have all of your side's strength, there is little risk that a falsecard on opening lead will damage partner. In other situations such a ploy is much more dangerous.

There are numerous defensive positions in which simply playing the normal card would leave declarer with no losing option. Here we enter the realm of what are known as 'obligatory' or 'automatic' falsecards. Such considerations obviously take precedence over all others. After all, there is little point in partner's knowing what you have if declarer cannot go wrong. Our next two hands illustrate two of the basic positions in which a defender *must* play a falsecard. The objective in both situations is to provide declarer with a losing option where none would exist if the defender played the 'normal' card.

```
Both Vul.          ♠  8 7 2
Lead: ♠K           ♥  A J 7 3
                   ♦  9 7
                   ♣  A K Q 6

♠  K Q 5 4              N              ♠  A 10 9
♥  K 2                                 ♥  10 9 4
♦  Q 8 6 5      W          E           ♦  J 10 4 3 2
♣  5 4 2                               ♣  9 7
                        S

                   ♠  J 6 3
                   ♥  Q 8 6 5
                   ♦  A K
                   ♣  J 10 8 3
```

WEST	NORTH	EAST	SOUTH
	1♣	pass	1♥
pass	2♥	pass	2NT
pass	4♥	all pass	

The defenders cash three rounds of spades and exit with a club. Declarer wins in dummy, crosses to the ♦K and plays a heart to dummy's jack. If East follows mechanically with the ♥4, then declarer has no option but to cash the ♥A and hope the ♥K comes down doubleton. But if East plays the ♥9 or the ♥10 under the jack, declarer has a choice on the second round of the suit. He may decide to cross back to hand with the ♦A and lead the ♥Q, attempting to pin the second card from ♥109 doubleton in the East hand.

This particular defensive ploy has a higher chance of success when the key suit is trumps, as here. Declarer must usually guess how to play the trump suit before he has a count of the other suits. If North-South had bid to 3NT on these cards, the defense would probably have started with four rounds of spades. Declarer then wins the diamond switch, plays a heart to the jack, and cashes four rounds of clubs. Having discovered that West had seven black cards to East's five, it would be clearer now for declarer to play West for the doubleton heart.

Our second hand on this theme features one of the most written-about obligatory falsecard positions. Although many readers will be familiar with this situation, it is worth looking at to see how declarer can try to force the defenders to play honestly:

The suit combination overleaf is one that many readers will be familiar with, and so we shall only deal with it very briefly from the defenders' angle. As we shall see though, that is only half of the story.

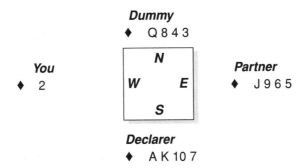

Dummy
♦ Q 8 4 3

You
♦ 2

Partner
♦ J 9 6 5

Declarer
♦ A K 10 7

It is normal for declarer to cash a high honor from his hand and then, if both defenders follow with low cards, to cross to dummy's queen in order to pick up ♠J9xx left, declarer can never make four spade tricks, but he can if East has that holding. East can see what is about to happen, and he has only one chance to deflect declarer from the inevitable, and winning, line of play — that is to play the♠9 on the first round of the suit. The result of this is that declarer now has a losing option. He can continue with his original plan or he can cash the second honor from his hand next, intending to finesse against West's jack if East shows out on the second round.

Now let's put this suit into a full deal to see how declarer might overcome such trickery. Perhaps there is a way for him to force the defenders to play honestly. To add a little spice, there is a grand slam riding on declarer's skill:

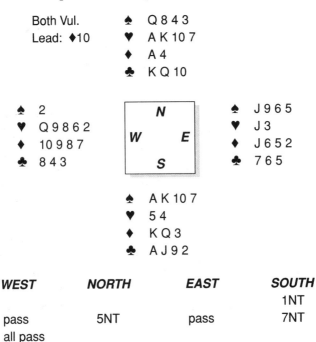

Both Vul.
Lead: ♦10

♠ Q 8 4 3
♥ A K 10 7
♦ A 4
♣ K Q 10

♠ 2
♥ Q 9 8 6 2
♦ 10 9 8 7
♣ 8 4 3

♠ J 9 6 5
♥ J 3
♦ J 6 5 2
♣ 7 6 5

♠ A K 10 7
♥ 5 4
♦ K Q 3
♣ A J 9 2

WEST	NORTH	EAST	SOUTH
			1NT
pass	5NT	pass	7NT
all pass			

Declarer wins the opening lead and plays two more rounds of diamonds followed by four rounds of clubs, both defenders discarding a diamond on the thirteenth club. Declarer now plays the ♠K. If East follows with the ♠5, declarer will next play a spade to the queen and subsequently pick up the suit. Why? Because if West has ♠J96 left, declarer can never score four spade tricks, but he can if East has that holding. To give declarer a losing option, East must follow with the ♠9 under the king. Declarer now has a choice, as he can pick up ♠J65 on either side. Having cashed his club and diamond winners, all declarer knows is that each defender started with seven minor-suit cards. There is no indication who is more likely to have a singleton spade. It's a guess — declarer has done all he can to get a count on this hand... Or has he?

Not at all. In fact, declarer has gone some way to creating this dilemma for himself. For a start, he should have won the diamond lead and cashed four club tricks immediately. It would then be far from obvious for both defenders to discard a diamond, and a major-suit discard would have made life much easier. Declarer had a second chance too — note the subtle difference if he cashes his minor-suit winners and then crosses to dummy in hearts to lead a spade towards his hand.

In the first scenario, when declarer leads the ♠K from hand, a good defender in the East seat knows he must play the nine as he has already seen his partner follow with the ♠2. When declarer leads the first round of spades from dummy, it is extremely dangerous for East to play the ♠9 from ♠J9xx since his partner might have the singleton ten. If that is the layout, then playing the ♠9 is the only way to let the contract make. If East does play the ♠9 when the suit is led from dummy, declarer should assume it is a singleton. If it transpires the ♠9 is from ♠J9xx, all declarer can do is congratulate East on a fine play and nerves of steel.

Subtlety is paramount when trying to deflect declarer from a normal line of play that is destined to succeed. For instance, if you have opened a 15-17 1NT it is pointless trying to persuade declarer that you have a 12-count. It is just not believable. Instead, you must try to make him think you have a *different* 15-17 point hand from the one you actually hold. Sometimes you will try to conceal a particular honor, so that declarer will play you for a high card that partner has. On other occasions, it will be your distribution that you will try to distort slightly. Note the word *slightly*. Declarer will never believe any attempted deception that is massively at variance with the bidding and/or the early play.

Preventing declarer from getting an accurate count of your distribution or disguising the defensive honor distribution can produce numerous benefits. Many apparently cold contracts fail because a defender offers declarer a choice of plays. Our next deal occurred at a Junior European Championship. Try it as a problem from declarer's seat:

Both Vul.
Lead: ♥7

♠ J 8 4
♥ A 6 3
♦ K 10 7 5
♣ K Q 6

```
        N
    W       E
        S
```

♠ A K 7 3
♥ J 10 4
♦ Q 8 2
♣ A J 5

WEST	NORTH	EAST	SOUTH
			1NT
pass	3NT	all pass	

The heart lead runs to East's ♥8 and your ♥J. You have eight tricks now, counting a diamond, and you need a second diamond or a third spade trick. Hearts appear to be 5-2, so you must also knock out West's entry early. You cross on a club and lead a diamond — the queen holds. If West has the ♠Q or if spades are 3-3, you don't need the diamond finesse, so you play a spade to the jack, losing to East's ♠Q. Hearts are continued; you win the third round of hearts with dummy's ace and East discards (a club). You cash spades, and when West has only two you have to fall back on a finesse against the ♦J. But...

♠ J 8 4
♥ A 6 3
♦ K 10 7 5
♣ K Q 6

♠ 9 2
♥ K Q 9 7 5
♦ A J 4
♣ 9 7 2

```
        N
    W       E
        S
```

♠ Q 10 6 5
♥ 8 2
♦ 9 6 3
♣ 10 8 4 3

♠ A K 7 3
♥ J 10 4
♦ Q 8 2
♣ A J 5

West wins the ♦A and cashes two hearts. One down! Clearly, if you simply play a second diamond after the ♦Q wins, you make your contract with an overtrick. But can you honestly say you would have done so? With the ♦J onside, West could count nine tricks for declarer if he took his ♦A. He didn't know exactly what would happen if he ducked the ♦A, but he could tell that winning the trick was giving up. Of course, when you make a play such as this, you must do so smoothly. If West had paused even for a fraction of a second before ducking the ♦A, the whole plan would have been lost.

On the next deal, the defender knows exactly what he is doing, and why. Take the West cards and see if you can avoid what appears to be your destiny:

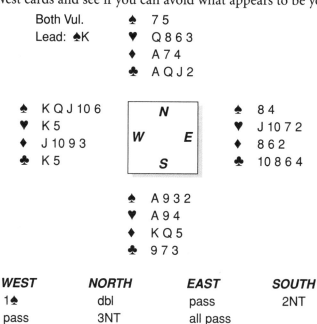

	Both Vul.	♠ 7 5
	Lead: ♠K	♥ Q 8 6 3
		♦ A 7 4
		♣ A Q J 2

WEST	NORTH	EAST	SOUTH
1♠	dbl	pass	2NT
pass	3NT	all pass	

Declarer ducks the first spade and wins the second with his ace as your partner plays high-low. After playing a club to the queen, declarer returns to his hand with ♦Q and plays a second club to your king and dummy's ace. You can see what is about to happen. Can you do anything about it?

Declarer plans to play off his minor-suit winners and throw you in on the third round of spades. You will make four spade tricks, but your last two cards will be ♥Kx and you will have to give declarer his ninth trick in hearts. Keeping the fourth diamond and only one spade winner doesn't help either.

Your only hope of avoiding this fate is to convince declarer that, instead of your actual 5-2-4-2 shape, you are 5-3-3-2. Most of your thinking must have been done well before the crucial moment — when declarer cashes dummy's ♣A. You must nonchalantly discard your small heart on this trick.

All that remains is to add the finishing touches to the picture that you are painting in declarer's mind. When he cashes his diamond winners, follow with the ♦10 and ♦J, hoping that declarer will be persuaded that your partner has the ♦9, confirming that you started with a 5-3-3-2 shape. He expects your last four cards to be two spade winners and ♥Kx. When he throws you in with a spade, you will take your spade winners. Then be sure to enjoy the look of horror on declarer's face when you produce the ♦9 at Trick 12.

As a final comment, it is worth noting that declarer would have done better to duck the second spade. It wouldn't have helped in any material way, but what do you think East would have discarded on the third round of spades? Our bet is that it would have been a small diamond. If that happened, East would then show out when declarer cashed the third diamond, completely destroying the masterpiece you were in the process of painting.

The next two hands illustrate what you might call desperation measures. In short, simple counting tells you that, if you sit there like a stuffed toy, declarer will make his contract. Your only hope is to produce a diversion, like a magician pulling a rabbit out of a hat, in the hope that an extra trick will materialize out of thin air. To find defensive plays of this kind you must visualize the entire hand. The first exhibit features a favorite trick of the late, great Irving Rose. If you feel up to testing your imaginative powers, take the East seat and cover the West and South cards.

```
        Neither Vul.     ♠  8
        Lead: ♠Q         ♥  Q 10 7
                         ♦  K J 10 7 4
                         ♣  A Q 8 3

  ♠  Q J 10 5       ┌─────────┐      ♠  A 9 7 2
  ♥  A 5            │    N    │      ♥  8 4 3
  ♦  A 6 5          │  W   E  │      ♦  Q 9
  ♣  K 10 7 4       │    S    │      ♣  9 6 5 2
                    └─────────┘

                         ♠  K 6 4 3
                         ♥  K J 9 6 2
                         ♦  8 3 2
                         ♣  J
```

WEST	NORTH	EAST	SOUTH
	1♦	pass	1♥
dbl	2♥	2♠	3♥
all pass			

After a competitive auction, partner leads the ♠Q to your ace. How do you plan to take five defensive tricks?

The lead places declarer with the ♠K, and his hearts must surely be headed by at least one top honor. Counting your potential defensive tricks, it is not easy to see more than the spade you already have, partner's presumed trump trick, and perhaps two diamonds. However, by playing a little game of 'What if...' you might come up with a route to a fifth trick.

Let's start with, 'What if partner's trump honor is the ace?' Then ask yourself, 'Can declarer have three diamonds?' Clearly, both are possible. If that is the layout, what do you think is likely to happen if you win the ♠A at Trick 1 and immediately fire back the ♦9?

Look at the whole hand and view things from declarer's seat. West wins the ♦A at Trick 2 and returns the suit. Wouldn't you play low? Wouldn't you be sure that East was about to ruff the second round of diamonds? It appears that your only chances are that West does not have the ♥A, or that East only has two trumps. This time though, East wins the ♦Q, puts his partner in with the ♥A and *now* gets his diamond ruff to defeat a contract that moments earlier seemed impregnable. On a technical note, it is worth mentioning that East should lead the ♥8 when putting partner in with his trump ace. This is a clear trump echo to let partner know that he wants a diamond ruff.

Our second example was a creation of the late Victor Mollo. Take the East hand and see if you can come up with the defense and the reasoning that Mollo attributed to the Hideous Hog:

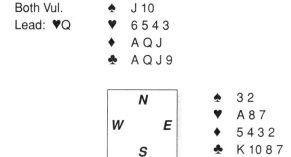

```
Both Vul.        ♠  J 10
Lead: ♥Q         ♥  6 5 4 3
                 ♦  A Q J
                 ♣  A Q J 9

                                  ♠  3 2
              N                   ♥  A 8 7
          W       E               ♦  5 4 3 2
              S                   ♣  K 10 8 7
```

WEST	NORTH	EAST	SOUTH
			pass
pass	1♣	pass	1♠
pass	1NT	pass	4♠
all pass			

You win the ♥A as declarer follows with the ten. What now?

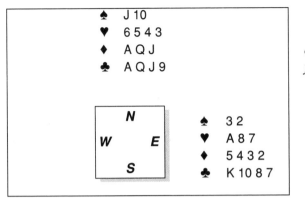

diagram repeated for convenience

You have one trick in, and expect to score the ♣K. South's initial pass and his subsequent jump to game suggest that he has six or seven trumps missing a top honor, so you can presume that partner has a trump winner for your third trick. Prospects for a fourth defensive trick look rather bleak, though. Your only chance of beating the contract is with a ruff — but in which suit?

The inimitable Hog returned a *club* — the ten, to be precise. Look at the full hand and consider things from declarer's point of view:

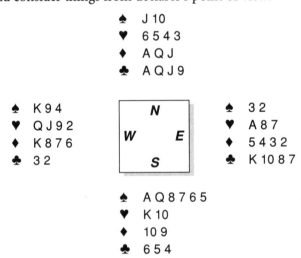

The heart lead goes to East's ace and the ♣10 is returned. Declarer wins in dummy, runs the ♠J to West's king and a second club is returned. It seems obvious that East's ♣10 was from shortness, but declarer can afford to lose a club ruff — he will win the return, draw trumps, and repeat the club finesse to discard his diamond loser. What he cannot afford is to have the ♣A ruffed. So declarer plays a low club from dummy, losing to the ♣K and *West* gets a club ruff! A very clever defense by East, for sure, and one that most declarers would surely fall for in practice.

What these hands illustrate is that if a count of the obvious defensive tricks reveals that you cannot beat the contract, then you must look for some way to lure declarer into a line of play that fails. For our final examples on the subject of painting a false picture of your hand, we concentrate on those rare occasions when the winning defense is to mislead your partner intentionally. Our first hand comes from the 1993 Venice Cup — the Women's World Team Championship. This was the layout of the heart suit that the British West could see:

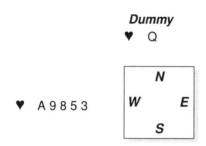

West, who had no entry outside the heart suit, led the ♥5 against 3NT. At Trick 1, East's king covered the queen and declarer followed with the ♥2. East returned the ♥6 and declarer played the ♥10. What would you do?

At the table West decided, not unreasonably, that the layout of the heart suit was like this:

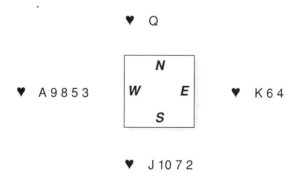

West ducked declarer's ♥10 so that, when East regained the lead, she could play her remaining heart through declarer's ♥Jx. Unfortunately, East did not gain the lead again until it was far too late. 'Too bad,' you may think — except that the actual heart position was:

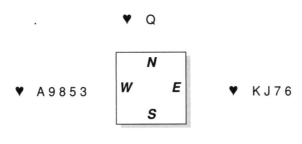

♥ Q

♥ A 9 8 5 3   **W**   **E**   ♥ K J 7 6

N

S

♥ 10 4 2

Note declarer's alert play of the ♥10 on the second round, which smacks of an old Rixi Markus saying: 'if you are going to duck, duck high.'

Many players would have made the same mistake as this East. After all, it has been second nature to us all since we were beginners to return the higher of two remaining cards and to play back the lowest with an original four-card holding. In this case, though, returning the jack can never be wrong. While it may initially mislead partner about your holding, by the time partner discovers she has been duped it is too late for her to do the wrong thing.

On our final deal, the correct defense requires East to have the foresight to realize that he must lie to his partner. The hand occurred at the 1997 Venice International Teams tournament. The unlucky declarer was Cezary Balicki of Poland and Italy's Massimo Lanzarotti held the East cards.

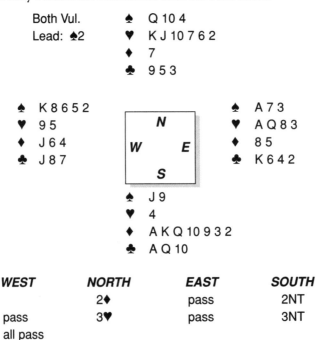

Both Vul.   ♠ Q 10 4
Lead: ♠2   ♥ K J 10 7 6 2
         ♦ 7
         ♣ 9 5 3

♠ K 8 6 5 2   ♠ A 7 3
♥ 9 5   **N**   ♥ A Q 8 3
♦ J 6 4   **W**   **E**   ♦ 8 5
♣ J 8 7   **S**   ♣ K 6 4 2

         ♠ J 9
         ♥ 4
         ♦ A K Q 10 9 3 2
         ♣ A Q 10

WEST	NORTH	EAST	SOUTH
	2♦	pass	2NT
pass	3♥	pass	3NT
all pass			

North's 2♦ opening was Multi, showing either a weak two in one of the majors or various strong hands. South's 2NT enquired and 3♥ showed a minimum weak two in hearts.

East-West's opening lead style was third and fifth, so East knew from the ♠2 that his partner had a five-card spade suit. Dummy played the ♠10, and double-dummy it is easy enough to see how the defense can make five tricks. Making it happen in practice is not so easy, though. Can you see how East forced his partner into the winning defense?

If East ducks Trick 1, declarer has nine easy tricks via a simple club finesse. If he wins and 'correctly' returns the standard ♠7, is it not likely that West will duck to maintain communications? Winning the ♠A and switching to a diamond does not work either — declarer wins, cashes his diamonds, and exits with the ♠J. Whichever defender wins the spade must now give declarer his ninth trick.

At the table, Lanzarotti found the only defense to make sure of beating the contract. He grabbed the ♠A and returned the *three* of spades! Seeing no future in spades (as his partner clearly had only a doubleton), West took his king and switched to a heart. East won the queen, cashed the ♥A, and exited with a diamond, leaving declarer to lead away from his ♣AQ at Trick 12. One down!

Lanzarotti's defense demonstrates incredible imagination. He had to envision the whole hand, with twenty-four unseen cards, and then take the responsibility to 'cheat' on his partner in order to force him into the winning defense. Now *that* is brilliant!

- Signal accurately when there is a chance that partner needs the information in order to find the correct defense.

- When *you* have all of the defensive assets, feel free to signal in any way you think is likely to mislead declarer.

- When *partner* has all of the defensive assets, be sure your signals are accurate.

- If you have the defense's long suit, protect your entry even if it gives declarer a chance to make a trick he could not otherwise make.

- In obligatory falsecard situations, giving declarer a losing option takes precedence over any requirement to keep partner in the picture.

- If a count of declarer's high cards and shape tells you the contract is unbeatable by force, seek to create a realistic but false picture of the defensive hands that may lead declarer to adopt a losing line of play.

- When you are trying to paint a false picture of your hand, you must make it a *believable* picture.

- Do not show declarer your hand!

Other bridge titles from Master Point Press

Partnership Bidding *A workbook* by Mary Paul
0-9698461-0-X   96 pp. PB   Can $ 9.95   US$7.95   UK£5.99
"A wonderfully useful book." *BRIDGE magazine*

There Must Be A Way... *52 challenging bridge hands* by Andrew Diosy
(foreword by Eddie Kantar)
0-9698461-1-8   96 pp. PB $ 9.95 US & Canada   UK£6.99
"Treat yourself to a gem of a book." *Eddie Kantar*

You Have to See This *52 more challenging bridge problems* by Andrew Diosy and
Linda Lee
0-9698461-9-3   96 pp PB   Can $12.95   US$ 9.95   UK£7.99
"A frustratingly enjoyable read." *ACBL Bulletin*

Tales out of School *'Bridge 101' and other stories* by David Silver
(foreword by Dorothy Hayden Truscott)
0-9698461-2-6   128 pp PB   Can $ 12.95 US$9.95 UK£6.99
"Hilarious." Alan Truscott, *New York Times*

A Study in Silver *A second collection of bridge stories* by David Silver
0-9698461-5-0   128 pp PB   Can $ 12.95   US$ 9.95   UK£6.99
"Every bridge book by Silver has a golden lining." *The Toronto Star*

Focus On Declarer Play by Danny Roth
0-9698461-3-4   128 pp PB   Can $ 12.95   US $9.95   UK£6.99
Focus On Defence by Danny Roth
0-9698461-4-2   128 pp PB   Can $ 12.95   US $9.95   UK£6.99
"Far and away Danny Roth's best work so far... Highly recommended for anyone
between bright novice and experienced tournament player." *Bridge Plus magazine.*

Focus on Bidding by Danny Roth
1-894154-06-1   160 pp PB   Can. $14.95 US$ 11.95 UK£7.99
"This is not a book about systems or conventions — it is a book about bidding, and
about the places we go wrong in the auction."

The Complete Book of BOLS Bridge Tips edited by Sally Brock
0-9698461-6-9   176 pp PB, many photographs   Can $ 24.95 US$17.95
"The quality of each and every tip is exceptional and we maintain that the book cannot fail to improve your bridge." *Australian Bridge*